Business Financial Information Secrets

Business Financial Information Secrets

How a Business Produces and Utilizes Critical Financial Information

Tage C. Tracy

WILEY

For general information on our other products and services or for technical support,
please contact our Customer Care Department within the United States at (800) 762-
2974, outside the United States at (317) 572-3993 or fax (317) 572-4002.

Wiley also publishes its books in a variety of electronic formats. Some content that
appears in print may not be available in electronic formats. For more information about
Wiley products, visit our web site at www.wiley.com.

Library of Congress Cataloging-in-Publication Data:

Names: Tracy, Tage C., author.
Title: Business financial information secrets : how a business produces and utilizes
critical financial information / Tage C. Tracy.
Description: Hoboken, New Jersey : Wiley, [2021] | Includes index.
Identifiers: LCCN 2021014561 (print) | LCCN 2021014562 (ebook) | ISBN
    9781119779001 (paperback) | ISBN 9781119779032 (adobe pdf) | ISBN
    9781119779056 (epub)
Subjects: LCSH: Financial statements. | Business enterprises—Finance.
Classification: LCC HF5681.B2 T735 2021 (print) | LCC HF5681.B2 (ebook) |
    DDC 658.15/12—dc23
LC record available at https://lccn.loc.gov/2021014561
LC ebook record available at https://lccn.loc.gov/2021014562

Cover Design: Wiley
Cover Image: © mucahiddinsenturk/Shutterstock
SKY10027261_052421

Contents

Preface

When we first entertained the idea of writing *Business Financial Information Secrets*, we were a bit apprehensive about the idea – but not for the reasons you might think. There is no question that the financial, accounting, and strategic business content and concepts covered in this book represent essential knowledge that business owners, executives, board members, managers, external analysts, lenders, investors, and similar parties must know and understand how to utilize as a strategic weapon in today's rapidly evolving and changing global economy. In fact, we have never been more bullish on the material presented in this book, along with our companion book, *How to Read a Financial Report*, ninth edition, as it represents "evergreen" business knowledge covering the subjects of business accounting, financing, capital management, and planning.

Rather, our concerns lay more with the macroeconomic and political environments that have, since the start of 2020, gripped and consumed the world, which has seen an unprecedented response by governments and central banks across the globe. To drive home our point, think about this fact for a moment: Since the birth of the United States of America's Central Bank, known as the Federal Reserve System (or simply the Fed) in 1913, it took approximately 95 years to accumulate approximately $1 trillion in assets on its balance sheet (and basically the same amount of currency). Over the past 12 years, from 2008 through 2020, the Fed's balance sheet has grown from roughly $1 trillion to approximately $7 trillion (7x growth) to combat two major economic corrections, including the Great Recession from 2008 through 2010 and the COVID-19 economic shock experienced starting in 2020. If this does not gain your attention (and concern), then layer on this fact as well: Total global debt was approximately $87 trillion at the end of the 2000 compared to a global GDP of roughly $50 trillion (representing a ratio of 174%). By the end of 2020, total global debt had risen to an unbelievable estimated figure of $277 trillion compared to an estimated global GDP of approximately $88 trillion for 2020 (representing a ratio of 315%). These trends are simply not sustainable, as the only real reason more and more debt can be absorbed is via historically low interest rates (now less than 1%

for most of the world's public debt issued by developed countries) combined with ultra-accommodative terms.

So why our apprehension, you may ask, as it would appear now more than ever that the material presented in this book represents critical knowledge? The answer lies in the fact that between Wall Street (via the Fed) and Washington (not to mention countries and their respective banks from around the world), the current mindset seems to be centered on giving away free money.

That is, if you believe the Fed and the federal government are on the right path by handing out free money via loans (if you can call them that) with no regard for whether a company, individual, public entity, and so on can repay the loan, then this book is not for you. There is no point in understanding critical financial information, reports, analyses, sources and uses of capital, cash flow, and so on, as with free money raining down like there is no tomorrow, why even bother? Just load up on debt, spend it rapidly in unproductive ventures, cry poor or blame someone else, and then request another loan (i.e., wash, rinse, repeat). Better yet, why even bother with having accountants, business analysts, financial officers, or even the IRS, as in this bizarre new world financial accountability is not required?

Okay, we know this is a certainly a reach and yes, we are being sarcastic, but given the current policies being implemented at both the monetary and fiscal levels, the question does have to be asked about the financial viability not just of businesses but, even more importantly, at the governmental and country levels as well. This is where we became enthralled with writing this book, as the concepts and material presented are even more important and relevant today than ever before for individuals, businesses, governments, and countries alike. Our position is simple in that proper accounting and financial reporting will always be an essential and critical function of every business operating in free markets and economies around the globe.

This book, along with *How to Read a Financial Report*, have been written to assist the reader in gaining the most complete and comprehensive understanding of how businesses produce, report, distribute, analyze, and use financial information. While *How to Read a Financial Report* is focused on external users and readers looking in (from the *outside in*), *Business Financial Information Secrets* is focused on internal producers and users of financial statements/information (from the *inside out*). A wide range of topics will be covered, specifically focused on the difference between externally prepared financial reports and statements and internally generated financial information, with additional attention placed on raising capital, managing cash and liquidity, and understanding how a business generates and consumes cash.

In summary, the material presented in this book does not represent a luxury (i.e., it is nice to understand this content), as for internal and external users of the financial information to succeed in today's business world, this book offers must-have knowledge. Further, and a concept that we harp on time and time again throughout this book, if you do not understand a business's cash flows and financial capital resources, you will most likely fail to understand its very bloodline that keeps it alive, in good times or bad. So fail here, and you are possibly placing the very existence of your business at risk.

And to leave you with one final thought before you dive headfirst into the book, a simple reference to a quote from a movie might help explain the current economic environment and risks present. In the movie *Jurassic Park*, Dr. Allan Grant realized that the power of life (in the form of dinosaurs finding a way to reproduce) was far greater than the control over "unauthorized" breeding trying to be administered by the fictitious corporation known as InGen. As he so eloquently noted (by confirming that Dr. Ian Malcom was also correct in his assessment), "life found a way." In the same respect, free markets will eventually find a way to function in an economically viable manner and be allowed to correct, adjust, and survive, as the central control being administered over the markets (by both the Fed and the federal government) will eventually give way to what will most likely be an extremely violent and painful correction – all in the name of Adam Smith's theory on markets and the invisible hand.

 That is, invisible forces will act in such a powerful way that the laws of supply, demand, and individual pressures will result in the natural flow of resources, capital, and price discovery (beyond anything the central planners can control).

We absolutely believe that this will be the case as, with most of the world's global economy now based on some form of capitalism, it will only be a matter of time before natural economic market forces find a way to not only survive but thrive moving forward. This book is designed to make sure you have at least a fundamental understanding of the basic principles of business financial information, what is needed, where it comes from, when it is needed, how it is used, and why it is so important!

Note: We have prepared all of the exhibits in this book as Excel worksheets, which can be requested via email, free of charge, by reaching out to tagetracy@cox.net.

Acknowledgments and Dedication

We would like to express our utmost thanks to John Wiley & Sons, Inc., (commonly referred to as Wiley) for their continued support of our quest to produce and distribute relevant, timely, and critical accounting, financial, and business planning content to assist readers around the globe. Wiley has been a trusted partner to me and my father for over 30 years, during which time 15 books (including updated editions and this current title) have been published in over a dozen different languages. Wiley's current team, led by Kevin Harreld and Susan Cerra, have been a pleasure to work with as their level of professionalism, experience, and knowledge in this space is unmatched. This rings especially true at the time of this publication given the significant economic, political, social, environmental, and global health challenges facing basically all businesses throughout the world.

Taking the lead role in authoring this book, I would like to dedicate this project to, first, my parents: my dad, who turned a spry 86 years old in late 2020, and my mom, who passed away in 2017. I cannot tell you how much invaluable guidance my dad has provided on the topic of writing books as he encouraged me to take over the family business a decade or so ago, and how many thanks I owe my mom for saving my ass by editing numerous college papers drafted decades past (a job thankfully taken over by Wiley's editing department). But the real thanks to my parents resides in providing me with the proper moral compass and ethics on which I have operated my own business for the past 25+ years and coauthored numerous books. In an era when economic, business, and political trust is in such short supply, I can only look back to the foundation my parents laid for me with profound gratitude.

And second, it would be extremely selfish of me not to offer my sincere and deepest thanks and love to my immediate family, including my wife and partner in crime Kristin, our eldest son Mitchel (next in line to take over the family business), our daughter Katrina (and her new husband Nicolas Small), and our youngest son Tanner (and his new wife Meredith Cahill).

Their impact on my career and understanding of the importance of effectively discussing and communicating subjects of extreme importance in a clear, concise, and easy-to-understand manner is a lesson they have taught me every day of my life, and which I will never forget.

Along this same line, I would like to extend an extra-special thanks to my wife of 35+ years, who has somehow put up with an old bean counter and business professional like myself, always willing to lend an ear and pretend to enjoy learning more about such lively and entertaining topics as accounting and finance. Maybe she was actually interested (doubtful) or maybe she just needed a bit of conversation to help her fall asleep at night (probably, as this is a running joke between the two of us), but whatever the case, she has always supported my endeavors, no matter how challenging, time-consuming, or "out there," with zero doubt and 100% confidence. Could anyone ask for a better wife, partner, or friend?

Tage C. Tracy

About the Author

Tage C. Tracy (pronounced "Tog"/Scandinavian descent) has, over the past 25+ years, operated a financial consulting firm focused on offering CFO/executive-level support and planning services to private companies on a fractional basis. These services include providing guidance and support with raising debt and equity capital, completing complex financial analysis, supporting risk management assessments, guiding accounting system designs and structuring, and being an integral part of the strategic business planning management functions. Tage specializes in providing these services to businesses operating at four distinct stages: (1) startups and business launches, (2) rapid growth, ramp, and expansion management, (3) strategic exit and acquisition preparedness and management, and (4) turnarounds, challenged environments, and survival techniques.

Tage is also an active author and has been the lead or coauthor with a total of seven books, including this most recent title, *Business Financial Information Secrets*. The other books Tage has coauthored (with his father, John A. Tracy) include *How to Read a Financial Report*, ninth edition, *How to Read a Financial Report* – Comprehensive Version, *Cash Flow for Dummies*, *Small Business Financial Management Kit for Dummies*, previous editions of *How to Read a Financial Report*, and *How to Manage Profit and Cash Flow*.

Tage received his baccalaureate in accounting in 1985 from the University of Colorado at Boulder with honors. Tage began his career with Coopers & Lybrand (today PricewaterhouseCoopers) and obtained his CPA certificate in the state of Colorado in 1987 (now inactive). Tage can be reached on his website http://financemakescents.com/ or directly at tagetracy@cox.net.

PART ONE

The *What, When, and Where* of Producing Best-in-Class Financial Information

CHAPTER 1

The Big Three Financial Statements

STARTING WITH A QUICK BACKSTORY

As we launch into the content and concepts presented throughout this book, I would like to begin by referring to a book my father and I coauthored, titled *How to Read a Financial Report* (now in its ninth edition). This book, first written by my father and published by Wiley over 30 years ago, has stood the test of time and represents one of the top "go-to" technical accounting and financial references used by businesses, colleges, and organizations around the world. The book has so much useful information that you will find several overlaps and references to key financial and accounting concepts discussed in this book. However, there are also significant differences between these books that at heart are centered in the following two items:

> ➤ First, our book *How to Read a Financial Report* is centered on the premise of an external party (e.g., an investor, lender, etc.) evaluating or analyzing an organization from the outside looking in. That is, all the financial and accounting information produced has been done with the understanding that the audience will be external, independent third parties who are not privy to the organization's internal operations

and related financial information and data. This represents a critical difference between this book and *How to Read a Financial Report* that will become evident moving through the material. The content of this book has been structured to look at financial and accounting information from the inside out with a heavy emphasis on business management (as opposed to adhering to guidelines, rules, and regulations established by external bodies or organizations such as the SEC).

➤ Second, *How to Read a Financial Report* is presented from more of a technical/accounting perspective or, for lack of a better term, a bit more black-and-white (as it relates to providing an understanding of accounting and financial concepts and how the big three financial statements are interconnected). This book is based on more of an internal business approach where, while it adheres to general or standard accounting rules and guidelines, its primary purpose is to assist with socializing accounting concepts, financial analyses and reporting strategies, and business planning from an internal operating or strategic perspective. Or, as I told my dad (a retired professor emeritus from the University of Colorado), "That is how you teach it in the classroom, but this is how it is done on the street."

So, with this said, let's launch into our first topic on the big three financial statements, as there is no better place to start, making sure you have a clear understanding of the role and importance of the balance sheet, income statement (aka profit-and-loss, or P&L), and statement of cash flows. Large or small, for-profit or non-profit, corporations, LLCs, partnerships, or sole proprietorships, governments, or private businesses, legal or illegal, it doesn't really matter, as this basic concept is always present. That is, all operating entities need to produce complete, accurate, reliable, and timely financial statements on which to base sound business decision-making.

THE FINANCIAL REPORTING BEDROCK

It should go without saying that business managers, company lenders and investors, regulatory agencies, and countless other parties need to clearly and concisely understand an organization's financial performance and results in a timely manner. This is common sense, no doubt, but you would be absolutely amazed at how often this basic concept is overlooked or, for lack of a better term, neglected, by even the senior-most executive management teams. Maybe it is a result of ignorance, not having enough time, or just being lazy, but as we start our discussion on the big three financial statements, it should become abundantly clear just how important all three primary financial statements are and the key role each one plays.

Before we dive into a more detailed analysis of each of the big three financial statements, a quick overview of each financial statement and the related purpose is warranted:

> *The balance sheet:* The financial condition of a business is communicated in an accounting report called the *balance sheet*. In its simplest form, the balance sheet reports the assets owned by a business, the liabilities owed by the business (to third parties), and the net ownership equity (assets minus liabilities), all at a point in time.

> *The income statement (AKA the Profit & Loss or just the P&L):* The financial performance of a business that reports and measures its profit- or loss-making activities is presented in an accounting report called the *income statement*. In its simplest form, the income statement reports sales, costs of goods sold, operating expenses, other expenses or income, and finally, whether a net profit or loss was generated and covers a period of time (e.g., 12-month period of 1/1/20 through 12/31/20).

> *The statement of cash flows:* Finally, the last of the big three financial statements, and often the most important (but least understood), is the *statement of cash flows*. In its simplest form, this financial statement reports a business's sources (i.e., how a business generates cash), uses (i.e., how a company consumes cash), and net change in cash. Similar to the income statement, the statement of cash flows covers a time period which is almost always consistent with the time period reported in the income statement.

It should be noted that alternative titles for these financial statements are common. For the balance sheet, alternatives include "statement of financial condition" or "statement of financial position." An income statement may be titled "statement of operations" or "earnings statement" as well as the profit & loss or, more simply, the P&L. For ease of presentation, we stick with the names *balance sheet* and *income statement* to be consistent throughout the book. The statement of cash flows is almost always called just that (but sometimes referred to as just a cash flow statement).

Finally, as you work your way through the book, please remember these definitions for frequently used terms and concepts:

> **Financial information:** The term *financial information* is used throughout the entire book and in its broadest sense includes basically all types of financial reports, financial statements, data, analyses, evaluations, assessments, and so on. For ease of reference and consistency, we simply use the term *financial information* in an all-encompassing meaning, apart from Chapter 2, where we present a discussion on the role and importance of preparing external financial reports and statements (which represent a selection or fraction of internally generated financial information).

> **Businesses:** As previously noted, all types of businesses, organizations, not-for-profits, government entities, and so on should produce financial statements on a periodic basis. Again, for ease of reference and consistency, when we refer to a *business* throughout the book, it is assumed to include any one of the entities identified.

> **Financial statements:** The term *financial statements*, in the plural, generally refers to a complete set that includes a balance sheet, an income statement, and a statement of cash flows as well as often implying that multiple years of financial statements will be presented. Informally, financial statements are called just "financials." In almost all cases the financial statements need to be supplemented with additional information, which is presented in *footnotes* and *supporting schedules*. One supporting schedule is very common – the *statement of changes in stockholders' (owners') equity*.

THE INCOME STATEMENT, AKA PROFIT AND LOSS (P&L)

First up, we will begin with the income statement, as, for most parties, this is the financial statement that is not only looked to first to quickly assess total sales generated (which is a common measurement of the "size" of a business) and whether a business made any money (i.e., a profit), but, maybe more importantly, is the financial statement that tends to be the most easily understood. Exhibit 1.1 provides an example of a standard externally presented income statement.

The income statement is read in a step-down manner, like walking down a set of stairs. At the top of the staircase, sales revenue is reported first.

EXHIBIT 1.1   Audited Income Statement

QW Example Tech., Inc.
Audited Financial Statements
For the Fiscal Year Ending
12/31/2020

Income Statement For the Twelve-Month Period Ending (all numbers in thousands)	FYE 12/31/2019	FYE 12/31/2020
Sales Revenue, Net	$53,747	$72,198
Costs of Goods Sold	($24,259)	($27,541)
Gross Profit	$29,488	$44,657
Operating Expenses:		
Selling, Marketing, & Promotional	$9,406	$13,357
Corporate General & Administrative	$7,500	$9,000
Research, Development, & Design	$10,749	$12,996
Depreciation & Amortization Expense	$1,814	$2,421
Total Operating Expenses	$29,469	$37,774
Operating Income (Loss)	$19	$6,883
Other Expenses (Income):		
Other Expenses, Income, & Discontinued Ops	$250	$2,000
Interest Expense	$150	$400
Total Other Expenses (Income)	$400	$2,400
Net Profit (Loss) before Income Taxes	($381)	$4,483
Income Tax Expense (benefit)	($133)	$1,569
Net Profit (Loss)	($248)	$2,914

Confidential - Property of QW Example Tech., Inc.

Sales revenue (AKA the "top line") is always reported first with costs of goods sold then reported to calculate gross profit.

Operating expenses are reported after gross profits and capture general company business expenses.

Finally, after all expenses are reported the company reports its net profit (or loss) often referred to as the "bottom line."

Then, as you proceed down each step, a deduction of one or more expenses is reported. The first step deducts the cost of goods (products) sold from the sales revenue of goods sold, which gives *gross profit* (also called *gross margin* – one of the few places you see the term *profit* in income statements). This measure of profit is called *gross* because many other expenses are not yet deducted.

Next, a broad category of general business expenses, often referred to as *operating expenses* or *selling, general, and administrative expenses*, are reported in the P&L. In our income statement example (Exhibit 1.1) you see four different operating expenses presented, including selling, marketing, and promotional; corporate general and administrative; followed by research, development, and design; and finally depreciation and amortization expense. When preparing external income statements, there is no set rule as to how many expenses must be presented but generally speaking, you will find that most external income statements attempt to avoid providing too much detail and limit the list to eight or less (unless the business had a very unusual year and elects to provide additional disclosures).

In our example, the reason we have chosen to disclose three specific expense "buckets" separately is for their importance.

> First, in today's hyper-technology-driven economy, investors are keenly focused on just how much a business spends on research, development, and design (an extremely important function). Since our sample company is a technology-based business, this expense bucket makes sense to report separately.

> Second, selling, marketing, and promotional expense is also highlighted to reflect the importance of just how much a business must spend to secure or capture customers and, ultimately, drive sales revenue. Marketing, promotional, and selling expenses often are separated from general and administration expenses, given their significance (from a dollar perspective) and importance in driving sales revenue.

> Third, you will notice that in our income statement example, we have elected to report depreciation and amortization expense (unique non-cash expenses) as a separate line item. The reason for this is that as we move through the book and highlight the importance of understanding the statement of cash flows, it is very convenient to segregate noncash expenses such as depreciation and amortization expense as a separate line item in the income statement. It should be noted that businesses may or may not report depreciation or amortization expense on a separate line in their income statements based on the concept of materiality (discussed in Chapter 5). We have elected to report depreciation and amortization as a unique expense to better help our readers understand its impact on earnings, cash flow, and the balance sheet.

The level of detail for expenses in income statements is flexible and is really dependent on the desires of the company's management team to report what they believe is the right balance of providing too much detail versus not enough. From a financial reporting standards perspective, the guidelines are somewhat loose on this point and left open for different levels of opinions.

Finally, we reach the bottom portion of the income statement where other expenses and income are reported. Interest expense on debt is deducted as well as other non-recurring-type expenses (e.g., in this case, a large loss was incurred for a discontinued operation), which generates earnings before income tax. The last step is to deduct income tax expense, which gives net income, the bottom line in the income statement. Undoubtedly, you have heard the term *bottom line* (but this slang is not used in financial statements), as well as *top line*, which refers to total sales revenue. Other terminology you should be aware of includes being in the "black" (generating a profit) or the "red" (incurring a loss).

Note: Publicly owned businesses are required to report earnings per share (EPS), which basically is annual net income divided by the number of capital stock shares or similar investment units. Privately owned businesses don't have to report EPS, but this figure may be useful to their stockholders.

To conclude our introduction with the income statement, three items should be kept in mind.

First, the income statement presented in Exhibit 1.1 has been structured for external presentation (as opposed to internal business analysis). We dive into the key differences and importance of income statements prepared for external versus internal parties in Chapter 2.

Second, it is important to note that of the big three financial statements, the income statement is the one that tends to be the most easily and often manipulated or subject to misstatement. The reason for this is that many parties tend to focus first (and only) on this financial statement (making it the main attraction), as well as that these same parties are often not nearly as well versed in understanding the balance sheet and statement of cash flows.

 Third, you will see multiple references to this all-important advice (throughout the book) which simply states – *Understand the income statement, trust the balance sheet, but most importantly, rely on the statement of cash flows.* As you work through the financial statements and this book, the importance of the state of cash flows will become increasingly clear.

THE BALANCE SHEET

The financial statement that is second in line is the balance sheet, which in its simplest form presents the *financial condition* of a business at a point in time (e.g., as of the fiscal year ending 12/31/20). Unlike the income statement, which presents a business's financial performance over a period of time, the balance sheet reports and summarizes a business's assets and liabilities, as well as the ownership interests in the residual of assets in excess of liabilities (referred to as owners' equity).

EXHIBIT 1.2   Audited Balance Sheet

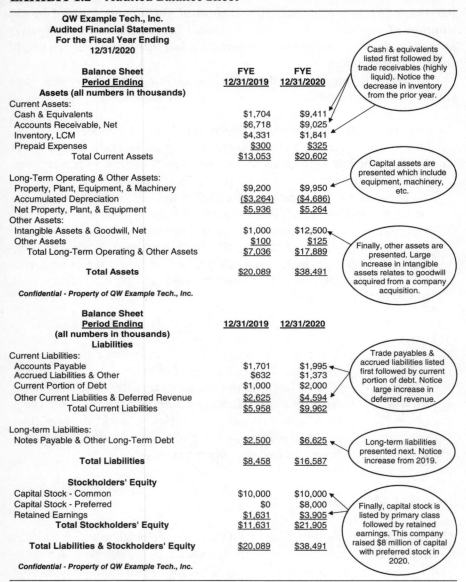

QW Example Tech., Inc.
Audited Financial Statements
For the Fiscal Year Ending
12/31/2020

Balance Sheet Period Ending	FYE 12/31/2019	FYE 12/31/2020
Assets (all numbers in thousands)		
Current Assets:		
Cash & Equivalents	$1,704	$9,411
Accounts Receivable, Net	$6,718	$9,025
Inventory, LCM	$4,331	$1,841
Prepaid Expenses	$300	$325
Total Current Assets	$13,053	$20,602
Long-Term Operating & Other Assets:		
Property, Plant, Equipment, & Machinery	$9,200	$9,950
Accumulated Depreciation	($3,264)	($4,686)
Net Property, Plant, & Equipment	$5,936	$5,264
Other Assets:		
Intangible Assets & Goodwill, Net	$1,000	$12,500
Other Assets	$100	$125
Total Long-Term Operating & Other Assets	$7,036	$17,889
Total Assets	$20,089	$38,491

Confidential - Property of QW Example Tech., Inc.

Balance Sheet Period Ending (all numbers in thousands)	12/31/2019	12/31/2020
Liabilities		
Current Liabilities:		
Accounts Payable	$1,701	$1,995
Accrued Liabilities & Other	$632	$1,373
Current Portion of Debt	$1,000	$2,000
Other Current Liabilities & Deferred Revenue	$2,625	$4,594
Total Current Liabilities	$5,958	$9,962
Long-term Liabilities:		
Notes Payable & Other Long-Term Debt	$2,500	$6,625
Total Liabilities	$8,458	$16,587
Stockholders' Equity		
Capital Stock - Common	$10,000	$10,000
Capital Stock - Preferred	$0	$8,000
Retained Earnings	$1,631	$3,905
Total Stockholders' Equity	$11,631	$21,905
Total Liabilities & Stockholders' Equity	$20,089	$38,491

Confidential - Property of QW Example Tech., Inc.

Callout annotations:
- Cash & equivalents listed first followed by trade receivables (highly liquid). Notice the decrease in inventory from the prior year.
- Capital assets are presented which include equipment, machinery, etc.
- Finally, other assets are presented. Large increase in intangible assets relates to goodwill acquired from a company acquisition.
- Trade payables & accrued liabilities listed first followed by current portion of debt. Notice large increase in deferred revenue.
- Long-term liabilities presented next. Notice increase from 2019.
- Finally, capital stock is listed by primary class followed by retained earnings. This company raised $8 million of capital with preferred stock in 2020.

The balance sheet shown in Exhibit 1.2 follows the standardized format regarding the classification and ordering of assets, liabilities, and ownership interests in the business. It should be noted that financial institutions, public utilities, railroads, and other specialized businesses use somewhat different balance sheet layouts but for the purpose of this book, we will use the standard format presented in Exhibit 1.2 for our overview. This format is generally used by technology companies, manufacturers, distributors, professional service companies, and retailers, as well as the large majority of other business types.

The assets, liabilities, and owners' equity reported in the balance sheet follow generally accepted conventions, which we briefly summarize here. According to long-standing rules, balance sheet accounts are subdivided into the following classes, or basic groups, in the following order of presentation:

Left Side (or Top Section)	Right Side (or Bottom Section)
Current assets	Current liabilities
Long-term operating assets	Long-term liabilities
Other assets	Owners' equity

Balance sheets are often presented in a horizontal format, with *assets* presented or listed on the left side, *liabilities* on the upper half of the right side, and *net owners' equity* on the lower half of the right side below the liabilities, to emphasize that the owners or equity holders in a business (the stockholders of a business corporation) have a secondary and lower-order claim on the assets – after its liabilities are satisfied. Balance sheets can also be presented in a vertical format with assets listed at the top or first, liabilities listed in the middle or second, and net owners' equity presented at the bottom or third. For ease of presentation, we used the vertical format in Exhibit 1.2.

Roughly speaking, a balance sheet lists assets in their order of "nearness to cash." Cash is listed first at the top of the assets stack. Next, receivables that will be collected in the short run are listed, and so on down the line. In later chapters, we say much more about the cash characteristics of different assets. In like manner, liabilities are presented in the sequence of their "nearness to payment." We discuss this point as we go along in later chapters.

Each separate asset, liability, and stockholders' equity reported in a balance sheet is called an *account*. Every account has a name (title) and a dollar amount, which is called its *balance*. For instance, from Exhibit 1.2, at the end of the most recent year ending 12/31/20 the inventory account had a balance of $1.841 million. It should be noted that the inventory account is most likely made up of multiple sub-accounts, including raw material, work-in-process, finished goods, and other inventory accounts, which for external reporting purposes are consolidated to reflect just one value in inventory.

This generally holds for most other balances (presented in the balance sheet); also, in almost all cases, the dollar figure represents a summation of multiple individual accounts (that are summed together given their similarities in purpose).

A balance sheet is prepared at the close of business on the last day of the income statement period. For example, if the income statement is for the year ending December 31, 2020, the balance sheet is prepared at midnight December 31, 2020. The amounts reported in the balance sheet are the balances of the accounts at that precise moment in time. The financial condition of the business is frozen for one split second. A business should be careful to make a precise and accurate cutoff to separate transactions between the period just ended and the next period.

A balance sheet does not report the flows of activities in the company's assets, liabilities, and shareowners' equity accounts during the period. Only the ending balances at the moment the balance sheet is prepared are reported for the accounts. For example, the company reports an ending cash balance of $9.441 million at the end of its most recent year (see again Exhibit 1.2). Can you tell the total cash inflows and outflows for the year? No, not from the balance sheet; you can't even get a clue from the balance sheet alone, as when understanding the flow of cash over a period of time, this represents the purpose of the statement of cash flows.

Some part of the total assets of a business comes not from liabilities but from its owners investing capital in the business and from retaining some or all of the profit the business earns that is not distributed to its owners. In this example the business is organized legally as a corporation. Its *stockholders' equity* accounts in the balance sheet reveal the sources of the company's total assets in excess of its total liabilities. Notice in Exhibit 1.2 the three stockholders' (owners') equity sources, which are called *capital stock – common*, *capital stock – preferred*, and *retained earnings*. The reason we have separated different forms of capital stock between common and preferred is extremely important to understand and will be covered in more depth in Chapter 17 in our discussion on sources of capital.

When owners (stockholders of a business corporation) invest capital in the business, the capital stock account is increased. Net income earned by a business less the amount distributed to owners increases the retained earnings account. The nature of retained earnings can be confusing; therefore, we explain this account in depth at the appropriate places in the book. Just a quick word of advice here: Retained earnings is *not*—we repeat, is *not*—an asset. Get such a notion out of your head.

A final word or two with the balance sheet. First, when reviewing the balance sheet, keep these thoughts in your head: Are your assets lying to you? and Are your liabilities telling you the truth? For example, in our balance sheet presented in Exhibit 1.2, the value in inventory as of the fiscal year-end 12/31/19 is stated at $4.331 million, yet this decreases to $1.841 million as of the fiscal year-end 12/31/20 (a substantial drop). The value of inventory was in fact written down in 2020 (as you will discover later in this book), but it begs the question, did management "massage" the inventory value to be a bit higher as of the fiscal year end 12/31/19 to protect net income?

Second, it is recommended that you become familiar with the term *balance sheet dressing.* No, this is not some special type of side dish served with your seasonal Thanksgiving Day turkey but rather represents the efforts by company executives to manage certain transactions as of the end of a period to present the performance of a business in the best light possible. When we dive into various company performance ratios and analyses covered in Chapters 8 and 9, this will become more apparent.

THE STATEMENT OF CASH FLOWS

Finally, we reach the third and final financial statement of the big three, which I like to think of in terms of the Disney movie *Cinderella.* If you recall, the two attention-starved stepsisters (i.e., the balance sheet and income statement) demand all the attention and relegate Cinderella to performing demeaning tasks. However, as the story moves forward, Cinderella blossoms into the most beautiful sister of all as her true, deep, and rich value comes to light. You might think of the statement of cash flows in this same light as, once you truly understand its importance and meaning, you will find that it really shines an amazing light on the operating performance of a business.

Okay, so this might be a bit of an overreach, but this analogy drives home a critical concept associated with the big three financial statements. That is, the income statement and, to a lesser extent, the balance sheet, tend to get most of the attention from financial experts, as in today's "time is of the essence" business mindset, the questions that generally first come to mind are: (a) What are top line sales (and how much did they grow)?, (b) What's the company's bottom-line profit?, and (c) How financially strong is the company? All good questions, but none of these addresses the most important question of all – can the business generate enough cash to support ongoing operations? This, in a nutshell, represents the essence of the statement of cash flows.

Earlier in this chapter you were introduced to the two hardcore financial statements that are included in the financial report of a business – Exhibit 1.1 (income statement) and Exhibit 1.2 (balance sheet). These two provide a comprehensive summary of the financial performance and financial condition of the business. This is not the end of the story, however. Financial reporting standards require that a *statement of cash flows* also be presented for the same time period as the income statement.

This third financial statement, as its title implies, focuses on the cash flows of the period. The cash flow statement is not "better" than the income statement and/or balance sheet. Rather, it discloses additional critical information that supplements the income statement and balance sheet.

EXHIBIT 1.3　Audited Statement of Cash Flows

QW Example Tech., Inc.
Audited Financial Statements
For the Fiscal Year Ending
12/31/2020

Statement of Cash Flows For the Twelve-Month Period Ending (all numbers in thousands)	FYE 12/31/2019	FYE 12/31/2020
Net Profit (Loss)	($248)	$2,914
Operating Activities, Cash provided (used):		
Depreciation & Amortization	$1,814	$2,421
Decrease (increase) in trade receivables	($746)	($2,307)
Decrease (increase) in inventory	$482	$2,490
Decrease (increase) in other current assets	($50)	($25)
Increase (decrease) in trade payables	$158	$294
Increase (decrease) in accrued liabilities	$68	$174
Increase (decrease) in other liabilities	$1,520	$2,536
Net Cash Flow from Operating Activities	$2,998	$8,497
Investing Activities, Cash provided (used):		
Capital Expenditures	($2,000)	($750)
Investments in Other Assets	$0	($12,525)
Net Cash Flow from Investing Activities	($2,000)	($13,275)
Financing Activities, Cash provided (used):		
Dividends or Distributions Paid	$0	($640)
Sale (repurchase) of Equity	$0	$8,000
Proceeds from Issuance of Debt	$0	$8,000
Repayments of Long-term Debt	($1,000)	($3,000)
Other Financing Activities	$250	$0
Net Cash Flow from Financing Activities	($750)	$12,360
Other Cash Flow Adjustments - Asset Impairment	$0	$125
Net Increase (decrease) in Cash & Equivalents	$247	$7,707
Beginning Cash & Equivalents Balance	$1,457	$1,704
Ending Cash & Equivalents Balance	$1,704	$9,411

Statement of cash flows begins with information from the income statement including net profit or loss & depr./amort. expense.

Net cash flow from operating activities presents a company's ability to generate or consume cash from internal operations.

Net cash flow from investing activities is presented next. Note the significant investment made in other assets (a business acquisition).

Net cash flow from financing activities is presented last. The company raised money from both debt and equity sources.

Ending cash balance agrees to the balance sheet (a proper check).

Exhibit 1.3 presents the statement of cash flows for our business example. Similar to the income statement, the statement of cash flows reads like going down a flight of stairs, from the top down, and has three primary parts, or layers: cash flows from *operating* activities, cash flows from *investing* activities, and cash flows from *financing* activities.

Cash flows from *operating activities* refers to revenue and expenses (as well as gains and losses) during the period that culminate in the bottom-line net income or loss for the period. In short, "operating" refers to the profit- (or loss-)making activities of the business and, as you can see, represents the first amount reported in the statement of cash flows (at the top of the statement). After this, companies generally report noncash expenses such as depreciation and amortization expense, along with reporting changes in the company's current assets and current liabilities realized during the reporting period. Once all this activity is reported, net cash flow from operating activities is reported, which in our example, amounts to a positive $8.497 million for the fiscal year ending 12/31/20.

Now this next statement may sound counterintuitive, but it is especially important to understand. That is, when a company's asset value increases over a period of time, this represents a use of cash (i.e., cash is consumed and decreases during the period). Likewise, when a company's asset value decreases over a period of time, this represents a source of cash (e.g., inventory is sold, the value is reduced, and it is turned into cash when the customer pays). On the liability side of life, a liability increasing in value over a period of time represents a source of cash (the opposite of the asset relationship), and a liability decreasing in value over a period of time represents a use of cash (e.g., vendor obligations due are paid, consuming cash).

As you work through the book, these concepts will become clearer and emphasize a critical concept in business financial management. That is, in order to improve liquidity and cash flows, businesses need to make sure they don't overinvest in assets (that consume excess cash) while at the same time utilize appropriate credit sources from vendors, third parties, future customers (e.g., receiving deposits), and so on to, for lack of a better term, leverage their liabilities to improve cash flows. Translation – what this really means is that smart business operators know exactly how far they can push vendors, suppliers, lenders, and so on to provide extra or extended terms to retain added cash inside a company to support ongoing operations.

Next up in the statement of cash flows is the section referred to as cash provided or (used) in *investing* activities. This section generally reports how a company spends or invests large amounts of cash/capital in long-term investments such as equipment or machinery additions, investments in intangible assets such as software development, and so forth (i.e., what long-term investments are being made by the company). In our sample company, one item that should clearly catch your eye is the $12.525 million investment made in other assets in the fiscal year ending 12/31/20. As we will discover later in the book, this investment was part of a large acquisition the company made of another business to drive future growth.

The final section in the statement of cash flows presents cash provided or used in the *financing* activities of the business. This section is designed to clearly disclose how a company finances its business operations from sources of cash other than operating cash flows (previously discussed). The information reported in this section relates to both how a company secures cash/capital (debt or equity) from external parties and how cash/capital is deployed as a return to the external parties. For example, in our sample company, you will notice that $8 million of new debt was secured in the fiscal year ending 12/31/20 while at the same time $3 million of old debt was repaid during the same period. You may ask what these transactions relate to, so I'll go ahead and give you a hint. The company raised new debt of $8 million (along with selling equity, raising another $8 million) to fund a large acquisition of approximately $12.5 million and as part of its new debt facility, the company was required to pay off an existing loan (thus the repayment or use of $3 million for debt).

At the very end of the statement of cash flows, a simple summary is provided that calculates the net increase or decrease in cash and adds this to the beginning cash balance, which then presents the final ending cash balance.

As we close our discussion on the statement of cash flows, it's worth visiting (and remembering) two critical concepts:

> First, you will notice that in our sample company, a net profit of $2.914 million was generated, compared to a net increase in cash of $7.707 million being realized during the year. So, if you've ever asked how the net increase in cash during a given period can be greater than the profit generated, the answer lies in the statement of cash flows. Rarely will you find a situation where the net profit generated equates to exactly the same amount of net cash increase during the same period as cash inflows from sales revenue are almost always higher or

lower than the actual sales revenue recorded during the period, and actual cash outflows for expenses are typically higher or lower than the amounts of expenses recorded for the period.

➢ Second, we would direct you toward our previous thoughts on understanding the income statement, trusting the balance sheet, and, most importantly, relying on the statement of cash flows. In effect, the statement of cash flows acts as the glue that ties or connects all the financial statements together. It starts by reporting net profit or loss and depreciation and amortization expense (both from the income statement). Then, it captures all the changes in a company's assets and liabilities to produce a net increase or decrease in cash, which, when added to the beginning cash balance, results in an ending cash balance (which ties to or should agree with the cash balance reported on the balance sheet). In effect, the statement of cash flows acts in the capacity of a self-regulating series of checks and balances to help parties better understand a company's economic model and ability to generate reliable positive cash flows (the ultimate purpose of a business).

CHAPTER 2

Externally Prepared Financial Statements and Reports

THE ROLE AND IMPORTANCE OF EXTERNAL FINANCIAL REPORTING

Before we dig deeper into our discussion on explaining the primary differences between internally generated financial information (starting in Chapter 3) and externally prepared financial reports and statements, an overview of the role and importance of externally prepared financial reporting is warranted. In the context of this chapter, when the term *financial information* is used, it is with the broadest meaning and includes reports, statements, analyses, evaluations, assessments, and so on (i.e., basically any type of internally generated financial data or information). This compares to externally produced financial information, which, for ease of understanding, includes financial statements and financial reports. Or, from a different perspective, internally generated financial information is all-encompassing, whereas externally produced financial reports and statements represent a selection or fraction of the financial information that management has elected to provide to external parties (either by choice or due to regulatory requirements).

As with internally generated financial information, the main purpose of external financial reporting is to provide up-to-date, complete, accurate, reliable, and timely financial information from a business to shareholders, investors, lenders, analysts, governmental agencies, credit bureaus, and the

19

like. In fact, an efficiently functioning accounting and financial information system, one that leverages both software/technology and company personnel resources, can achieve the dual mandate of producing financial information for both external and internal consumption (in a cost-effective manner).

It should be obvious that investors and lenders are straightforward examples of external parties requiring access to financial information as they represent potential sources of capital (debt and equity) to support a business's ongoing operations. As such, they have a right to and need for financial information. Other parties are also interested in the financial affairs of a business—for example, its employees, other creditors, analysts (who provide independent assessments of a business), regulatory groups, governmental agencies, and so on. When external parties read financial reports that are made public, they should keep in mind that these communications are primarily directed to the owner-investors of the business and its lenders (i.e., the primary capital sources). External financial reporting standards that are utilized to prepare and provide financial information to the public have been developed with this primary audience in mind.

A quick word of caution as it relates to the term *public*: When we use this term, any financial information that is provided to the public can be accessed by basically any third party. This could be a financial analyst, a governmental entity, a competing business, or an investor or day trader plying their trade on Robinhood. If they know where to access the information, any party can gain rather detailed insight into a business.

According to estimates, there were over 8,000 publicly traded companies on the U.S. stock exchanges in the mid-1990s. Since then, by 2016, this number had decreased to just 3,600 publicly owned businesses in the United States but rebounded to approximately 6,000 by 2020. Their capital stock shares and other securities are traded in public markets. The dissemination of financial information by these companies is governed by federal law, which is enforced mainly by the Securities and Exchange Commission (SEC). The New York Stock Exchange, Nasdaq, and Internet securities markets also enforce rules and regulations over the communication of financial information by companies whose securities are traded on their markets.

Securities of foreign businesses are traded in stock markets around the world. Many countries, including the United States, have been attempting to develop a set of *international financial reporting and accounting standards*. This process has not gone as smoothly as many had hoped. Indeed, at the time of this writing (2020), the SEC has not yet given its formal endorsement of international standards. U.S. businesses are not yet required to adopt the global standards.

In the United States and other countries, public companies cannot legally release information to some stockholders or lenders but not to others, nor can a business tip off some of them before informing the others. The laws and established standards of financial reporting are designed to ensure that all stockholders, analysts, and lenders have equal access to a company's financial information and financial reports.

A company's financial report may not be the first source of information about its profit performance. In the United States, most public corporations issue press releases of their most recent earnings results, but it is important to remember that the releases of the earnings may not have been audited by an independent CPA firm. These press releases precede the mailing of hard copies of the company's financial report to its stockholders, lenders, and other parties. Most public companies put their financial reports on their websites at the time of or soon after the press releases. Private businesses do not usually send out letters to their owners and lenders in advance of their financial reports, although they could. As a rule, private companies do not put their financial reports on publicly accessible websites.

PRIMARY EXTERNAL REPORTING DRIVERS

Basically, the need for external reporting comes down to one of two primary drivers – *taxation and compliance* and *capital sources* (as we have previously highlighted):

1. *Taxation and compliance:* Most people realize that there is a significant demand for financial reporting because of income taxes. Whether it is at the federal (i.e., IRS) or state (e.g., the Franchise Tax Board in California) level, it goes without saying that financial reporting of operating results to tax authorities is generally not the most eagerly anticipated task on an annual basis. It is important to remember that beyond income tax reporting, a vast requirement is present to report financial information to other organizations (primarily governmental) that involve many different taxes and financial data needs. Quite honestly, income tax reporting often is the least worrisome tax compliance requirement, as once a business expands and begins to operate in multiple states and foreign countries, a bevy of additional tax reporting is required, including payroll (for both employees and consultants), sales and use taxes (a hot issue because of ecommerce business models), property taxes, excise taxes, and others. But let us not stop here as, in addition to reporting

financial information for different types of business taxes, there is a large demand for financial data from other regulatory organizations as well. Any business operating in government contracting realizes this, as having to validate prevailing wage compensation (remitted to employees) or adhering to product or service pricing that is governed by strict agreements is par for the course. The list of potential nontaxation financial reporting requirements is endless and tends to vary by industry but the point that needs to be made is simple. Governmental data and financial reporting requirements are extensive and, without a properly functioning accounting and financial reporting system (refer to Chapter 5 on accuracy and reliability), businesses will undoubtedly waste time, effort, and money.

2. *Capital sources:* In Chapters 13 and 17 we will dive into a deeper discussion on different forms, types, and structures of business financial capital sources, but to start, external business financial capital basically comes from one of two sources – equity or debt. When thinking of equity, public companies are the obvious reference here given the slew of financial reporting that needs to be made available publicly. This includes the need to report financial results on an annual (referred to as a 10K) or quarterly (referred to as a 10Q) basis via issuing reports to the Securities and Exchange Commission (SEC). These reports are required reporting for public companies but the need for external financial reporting does not stop with public companies. Most private businesses and organizations must also report financial results to investors, owners, lenders (such as banks or leasing companies), board members, and other similar parties. The sheer volume of the different types of financial reports and statements that may be requested makes it impossible to list them in this book, but the basic premise is simple: If a third party is going to invest financial capital in your business (equity or debt), then you can be assured that external financial reporting will be required.

In trying to simplify our discussion as to the parties requiring external financial reporting and main drivers demanding business financial information, we might leave you with these three tidbits of advice:

➤ First, basically every government entity, including states, counties, and cities, is hungry for tax receipts in the current economic environment (which is being amplified by the COVID-19 pandemic). It would be wise to become familiar with the acronym SALT (state and local taxation) as, while the federal government presents enough challenges with taxation, just wait until you must deal with 20+ states, all with different rules, regulations, and reporting requirements. And if you need any proof of just how daunting this can be, please brief yourself on *South Dakota v. Wayfair*, which basically paves the way for states to require businesses, even without establishing a nexus or having a physical place of business in the state, to charge, collect, and remit sales tax for the sale of specific goods and services. Given the shift toward ecommerce and the demise of traditional retail, it does not take a genius to figure out how much sales tax revenue states have been losing over the past decade.

Second, remember this all-important statement – Less is more! What we mean by this is that when reporting to external parties, for whatever need, focus on providing the external party with the specific information requested, in the desired/preferred report format, no more and no less. The reason for this is simple. If you provide any type of excess information, reports, data, and so on, you are only going to open up Pandora's box, as not only are you going to confuse the requesting party but even more problematic, you are going to potentially invite them into areas of your business that they do not have any reason to be involved with. So, in the spirit of Less is More, also remember this all-important acronym – KISS (keep it simple, stupid), as keeping the information as simple as possible for the receiving party will make both your and their lives much easier.

> Third, understand the difference between public information and public entities demanding financial information. We previously noted that publicly traded companies are required to prepare financial reports to be made available to the general public. This should not be confused with preparing financial information for public entities (e.g., taxing authorities) that should remain confidential and not available to the general public. Unlike an annual report issued by Apple, Inc., which is readily available to all interested parties, Apple's annual federal income tax return is confidential and should remain private (under the control of the IRS).

THE FINANCIAL REPORT VERSUS FINANCIAL STATEMENTS

To further our discussion on externally prepared financial reports and statements, we would like to help further clarify the difference between the purpose and function of financial statements versus a company financial report. In this context, we are referring to a publicly traded company that is required, by regulatory bodies such as the SEC, to issue a quarterly or annual financial report.

It is important to keep in mind that while a company's financial statements represent the backbone for analyzing and evaluating its financial performance, financial reports include extensive additional financial, business, legal, and regulatory material that accompany the financial statements. The actual financial statements may take up anywhere from three to six pages of an external business financial report. But the complete financial report may often exceed 100 pages (compliments of management providing their discussion/assessment of operating results, along with the required financial statements' footnotes that accompany audited financial statements).

Although the remainder of the book is focused on producing and analyzing internally generated financial information, understanding what additional content and data is presented in financial reports (and why) makes sense, with our focus being on two primary tranches of additional information, including management discretionary disclosures and financial statement footnotes.

1. **Management discussion of operating results (MDOR):** The MDOR, sometimes referred to as the MD&A (management discussion and analysis), is a section of a business's financial report that is generally reserved for management to provide an assessment or overview of key operating results, market trends, industry data, strategies, and so on that management believes would be beneficial to external parties to help them more fully understand the operating results of a business. The MDOR is usually located at the front of the periodically prepared externally distributed financial report and quite often starts with a shareholder or investor letter prepared by the company's chairman of the board or CEO, for example. There is no doubt that the MDOR can provide useful information to external parties, but it should be noted that generally speaking, the information provided in the MDOR has

not been audited by the independent CPA firm (but rather represents information being presented by a company's management team). Translation: The MDOR tends to include a broader range of business information that has been internally prepared by the company and incorporates more "opinions" and "perspectives" than audited financial statements (which tend to stay factual in nature).

2. **Financial statement footnotes:** In contrast to MDOR disclosures, financial statement footnotes are part of the audited financial statements, prepared by an independent CPA firm (with support from company financial executives and legal counsel), and are most often located toward the back of the externally prepared financial report, just after the financial statements. The goal of financial statement footnotes is to provide additional clarity, support, and detail to validate and substantiate the information provided in the financial statements. For example, if a company has established a reserve for a potential liability due to uncertain legal actions brought against the company, the footnote will help shed additional light on the nature of the legal action and potential damages. Financial statement footnotes tend to avoid presenting management opinions and rather are more focused on sticking to the facts. Yet even here we must again point out an irony in the accounting and financial reporting world; that is, while the purpose of audited financial statements and associated footnotes is to present external financial reports, prepared by independent third-party CPAs, that are factual in nature, almost all audited financial statements and associated footnotes rely heavily on the use of estimates when calculating operating results. This concept underscores the importance of remembering that accounting is often just as much an art form as a science! In short, footnotes are the fourth essential part of every CPA-prepared or -audited financial report. Financial statements would be naked without their footnotes. This chapter explains the importance of reading the footnotes and some challenges and problems with footnotes. Studying a financial report should always include reading the footnotes to the financial statements.

In summary, it is important to remember that this chapter refers to information as presented in *external* financial reports—those that circulate outside the business. These financial reports and communications are designed mainly for use by outside business shareowners, analysts, company lenders, governmental agencies, and the like, with the business shareowners and lenders representing the two primary *stakeholders* in the business. Inside business executives, managers, and staff have access to significantly more information than that released in the company's external financial reports. This information is incredibly detailed in nature and is usually highly confidential, so external disclosure is tightly guarded. Diving into a more thorough discussion on internal business information will represent the balance of this book and is supported by the words of wisdom bestowed on us by Mr. Warren Buffett (when analyzing financial information) – the devil is in the details – so it goes without saying that invaluable internal financial information is both highly sought after and closely guarded, given its importance.

TYPES OF EXTERNALLY PREPARED FINANCIAL STATEMENTS

This chapter's final topic centers around the external financial statement reporting options that are most frequently utilized by company management to present financial statements to external parties. To start, we would like to drive home an important concept related to externally prepared financial statements versus reports. That is, for many private companies, there is no need to prepare and issue an entire financial report (as required by the SEC), as providing just the financial statements (along with financial footnotes when appropriate) is more than adequate. It should be obvious that providing financial statements is much quicker and cheaper than going to the trouble of providing a complete financial report; even for the external parties, it represents a more efficient process, as everyone can simply cut to the chase when analyzing a company's financial results.

Issuing external financial statements basically comes down to one of four choices, three of which are most often produced from retaining an independent CPA firm to prepare the financial statements (and include the following):

1. ***Compiled financial statements:*** Compiled financial statements are really nothing more than a CPA firm's taking company-prepared financial statements, formatting the information for external presentation, and then slapping the report on the CPA firm's letterhead; that's about it. Further, the CPA firm will not attest to the reliability of the compiled financial statements (being prepared in accordance with GAAP) and almost never attach or include financial statement

footnotes. If it hasn't already occurred to you, compiled financial statements are basically a joke, as almost no serious business utilizes this type of financial statement reporting.

2. ***Reviewed financial statements:*** For smaller to medium-sized businesses, reviewed financial statements are frequently prepared and utilized for external reporting purposes (as they are much lower in cost, easier to produce, and often satisfy external capital source reporting requirements). Reviewed financial statements are usually prepared by an independent CPA firm and involve the CPA's completing a more thorough evaluation of a company's financial performance using various analytical and financial analysis procedures. The CPA firm will attempt to present the financial statements in accordance with GAAP and generally will attach and include financial statement footnotes. It should be noted that the CPA firm will issue a review report that clearly states that they have not audited the company's financial information and, as such, do not guarantee compliance with GAAP (or other similar accounting frameworks). However, the review report will often make a statement that provides limited assurance that the company's financial statements are in compliance with GAAP without knowledge of any material modifications. Reviewed financial statements are much better than compiled financial statements but are not at the same level as audited financial statements.

3. ***Audited financial statements:*** Independent CPA firm–audited financial statements are without question the most reliable and comprehensive but also are the most time-consuming to prepare, expensive, and often the most complex. As previously noted, all publicly traded companies must have audited financial statements prepared and issued at least annually but it should be noted that countless other private businesses, governmental organizations, not-for-profit entities, and so on also have audited financial statements prepared. The reason for this is simple. The larger and more complex the reporting entity, the greater the demand for independent CPA firm audits to be completed. For example, a not-for-profit that receives $5 million a year in annual contributions may get by with having reviewed financial statements prepared, as the financial risks are relatively small compared to a group such as the Salvation Army, which raised approximately $150 million in 2019 and makes statements as to how much of each dollar raised is dedicated to program services (something large donors absolutely want verified).

If you recall, we referred to four types of financial statements being available for external presentation, which we have not forgotten about. The fourth type of financial statement is internally prepared financial statements (formatted or structured for external distribution). That is, a company can issue internally prepared financial statements that have not been reviewed, audited, evaluated, or analyzed by any third party or CPA firm. Rather, the company simply prepares the financial statements and issues them to the various third parties requesting the financial information.

In the private sector, you would be amazed (especially with smaller and medium-sized businesses) how often internally prepared financial statements are issued and accepted by external parties such as banks, investors, other lenders and creditors, and so on. There are several reasons why internally prepared financial information is the preferred route; they include cost (reviews and audits can be expensive), speed or timeliness (much quicker to produce and issue), simplicity (complex accounting issues are limited), and management credibility (third parties have a high degree of trust in the management team), to name a few. Whatever the reason, issuing internally prepared financial information to external parties is a quite common practice in the private sector and if this is indeed the path chosen, two key disclosures should always be made:

- First, a clear reference needs to be made stating that the financial information is unaudited and has been prepared by company management.
- Second, equally important, is that the following statement should always appear on this financial information: "Confidential, Property of XYZ Corporation."

By the way, we cannot pass on the opportunity to take a shot at the IRS and comment on the fact that many small companies often rely on issuing just their income tax returns to external parties for review (when requested). For many small companies, annual income tax returns often represent the only financial statements or information prepared on a periodic basis. In effect, this strategy represents the same concept as issuing internally prepared financial information to external parties but uses IRS forms and guidelines to report operating results.

There are a plethora of problems with providing income tax returns to external parties for review (to report financial information), including that the information is poorly structured, the IRS format is sorely outdated, there is no statement of cash flows presented, the method of reporting operating results may be misleading (e.g., cash basis of reporting is utilized, which is generally worthless), income tax returns may take over six months to prepare, income tax returns may contain highly confidential information, and the list goes on and on. But above all, it should be noted that taxing authorities request financial information in a structure and format that meets their needs (for compliance and governmental use) and not yours or any of your capital partners.

Relying on annual income tax returns (to support business decisions) is not recommended and is clearly not a prudent financial reporting strategy, as all businesses need to develop and implement proper financial information and reporting strategies on which to evaluate operating results – period!

CHAPTER 3

Internally Generated Financial Information

THE SHOTGUN VERSUS THE RIFLE

In Chapter 1, an overview was provided of the big three financial statements – the income statement, balance sheet, and statement of cash flows – which was followed in Chapter 2 by an explanation of the importance and role of external financial reporting. When examples of the financial statements were provided in Chapter 1 (and referenced in Chapter 2), they were done in the context of presenting them for use by a wide range of external parties (i.e., how financial statements are formatted and presented to parties who are independent or external to the business). In other words, let's use a shotgun approach to externally distribute standard financial information to a large and diverse potential audience.

Now with this topic out of the way and assuming you understand the importance and role of external financial reporting, let us turn our attention to generating internal financial information. Notice the broad reference to financial information, as for internal purposes it is not necessary to prepare complete financial statements for each specific management need or request. In fact, while complete financial statements should always be prepared, the distribution of these financial statements is generally reserved for the senior or executive management team (i.e., the parties who are responsible for all financial operating results of the company).

The norm for most companies is to prepare key financial information based on the needs or requirements of their internal audience. For example, a division manager may only see a sales flash report or a "short" P&L that captures the financial performance for this operating division (as opposed to the entire company's financial results). Thus, this represents the rifle approach as the goal is to deliver specifically tailored financial information to a targeted or narrow audience.

The reason for using this rifle strategy is twofold – focus and confidentiality. Businesses want to ensure that key management team members remain focused on achieving their targeted performance objectives and avoid distracting them with other business operations that they have no control or influence over. In addition, business financial information can be just as confidential inside a company or when distributed to external parties. A perfect example of this is centered in how key management team members are compensated, including any potential bonuses earned on achieving performance objectives. If bonus plans were made available to all management team members, you can imagine the potential problems that might arise within an organization from everyone wanting the best perceived plan available.

The purpose of this chapter and the remainder of the book is to pivot our discussion and focus on generating, presenting, and evaluating financial information for internal management use and analysis. I will pass along one spoiler alert, which should be both obvious and logical. The result of a financial statement, whether it be a balance sheet, income statement, or statement of cash flows, will be the exact same; that is, total assets reported in the balance sheet will be the same, the net profit or loss reported in the income statement will be the same, and the ending cash balance reported in the statement of cash flows will be the same. What will be different basically boils down to understanding five key items – format, detail, confidentiality, timeliness, and completeness.

THE BASICS OF GENERATING INTERNAL FINANCIAL INFORMATION

The best way to gain an understanding of the difference between external and internal financial reporting is to dive right in and view our fictitious company's internal income statement, presented in Exhibit 3.1.

EXHIBIT 3.1 Unaudited Internal Income Statement

Unaudited - Prepared by Company Management

QW Example Tech., Inc.
Unaudited Financial Statements
For the Fiscal Year Ending
12/31/2020

Income Statement for the Fiscal Year Ending	12/31/2019	% of Net Rev.	12/31/2020	% of Net Rev.
Revenue:				
Software Platform & SAAS Sales	$31,500,000	58.61%	$55,125,000	76.35%
Product Sales	$23,625,000	43.96%	$20,081,250	27.81%
Other Sales, Discounts, & Allowances	($1,378,000)	-2.56%	($3,008,000)	-4.17%
Net Revenue	$53,747,000	100.00%	$72,198,250	100.00%
Costs of Goods Sold:				
Direct Product Costs	$12,994,000	24.18%	$11,045,000	15.30%
Wages & Burden	$10,395,000	19.34%	$15,711,000	21.76%
Direct Overhead	$800,000	1.49%	$700,000	0.97%
Other Costs of Goods Sold	$70,000	0.13%	$85,000	0.12%
Total Costs of Goods Sold	$24,259,000	45.14%	$27,541,000	38.15%
Gross Profit	$29,488,000	54.86%	$44,657,250	61.85%
Gross Margin	54.86%		61.85%	
Direct Operating Expenses:				
Advertising, Promotional, & Selling	$4,232,700	7.88%	$6,010,650	8.33%
Personnel Wages, Burden, & Compensation	$3,056,950	5.69%	$4,674,950	6.48%
Facility Operating Expenses	$5,250,000	9.77%	$6,300,000	8.73%
Other Operating Expenses	$375,000	0.70%	$450,000	0.62%
Total Direct Operating Expenses	$12,914,650	24.03%	$17,435,600	24.15%
Contribution Profit	$16,573,350	30.84%	$27,221,650	37.70%
Contribution Margin	30.84%		37.70%	
Corporate Expenses & Overhead:				
Corporate Marketing, Branding, & Promotional	$2,116,350	3.94%	$2,671,400	3.70%
Research, Development, & Design	$10,749,000	20.00%	$12,996,000	18.00%
Corporate Overhead & Support	$1,875,000	3.49%	$2,250,000	3.12%
Depreciation & Amortization Expense	$1,814,286	3.38%	$2,421,429	3.35%
Total Operating Expenses	$16,554,636	30.80%	$20,338,829	28.17%
Operating Income (EBIT)	$18,714	0.03%	$6,882,821	9.53%
Operating Margin (EBIT Margin)	0.03%		9.53%	
Other Expenses (Income):				
Other Expenses, Income, & Discontinued Ops.	$250,000	0.47%	$2,000,000	2.77%
Interest Expense	$150,000	0.28%	$400,000	0.55%
Total Other Expenses (Income)	$400,000	0.74%	$2,400,000	3.32%
Net Income (Loss) Before Taxes	($381,286)	-0.71%	$4,482,821	6.21%
Income Tax Expense (Benefit)	($133,000)	-0.25%	$1,569,000	2.17%
Net Income (Loss) After Taxes	($248,286)	-0.46%	$2,913,821	4.04%

Confidential - Property of QW Example Tech., Inc.

Callout notes:
- Notice inclusion of a analytical ratio analysis.
- We now have far more detail related to the primary types of sales and costs of goods sold are split between major categories.
- Look at the level of detail now as we can understand exactly how much is being spent on different types of company selling & marketing expenses as well as facility versus

For ease of presentation of Exhibit 3.1, we have included just the income statement for the fiscal years ending 12/31/19 & 12/31/20, but similar income statements should be available for all company operating periods. As you can see, there are significant differences in the presentation of the financial information, which, as we noted earlier, boil down to five primary areas:

1. Format: The format should be much more user- and management-friendly (to drive home key points) as dictated by the company and not driven by external guidelines such as those of the IRS or SEC. We want to strike a proper balance between providing too much information (pushing the user toward "getting lost in the forest")

versus not enough, as the idea is to give the reviewing party what they ask for and need (based on their level of responsibility). Further, we do not want to divulge data that a party does not need or understand, that will confuse them, and/or is confidential (translation – above their security clearance, so to speak). Remember that most readers are not sophisticated accounting and financial professionals but do understand basic math, so the goal with the format is to provide financial information in the easiest-to-understand and reliable manner.

2. Detail: Obviously, the level of detail presented is far greater. In Exhibit 3.1, you can see that marketing, selling, advertising, and promotional expenses have been split between direct operating expenses and corporate costs. The difference between these two expense groups is that direct operating advertising and selling expenses capture what are commonly referred to as "call to action" expenses that are designed to turn a prospect into an actual customer (by placing an order). Corporate marketing and branding expenses represent a broader range of costs designed to help build awareness of the business and enhance its brand. For most businesses, understanding the difference between these two expense groups is especially important.

3. Confidentiality: The information presented in Exhibit 3.1 is highly confidential and needs to be controlled and safeguarded from not just external parties and prying eyes (e.g., a competitor) but also from internal parties (who may not understand the financial information and accidently disclose it to an unwanted party). Companies are always attempting to manage the delicate balance between disclosing extremely sensitive information (that is confidential and valuable) to external parties who help them accurately assess the operating results but at the same time not providing too much detail.

4. Timeliness: With internal financial information, quick is not an option; it is a necessity, including for full financial statements as, for company management team members, financial statements are generally prepared, distributed, and analyzed well in advance of issuing external financial statements and reports. This is done for two reasons. First, it gives key management team members an opportunity to evaluate the results and identify any potential errors, mistakes, or omissions. Second, if either good or bad news needs to be delivered to external parties, it provides the management team an

opportunity to prepare for the inevitable "grilling" that will be forth-coming. It should be noted that speed in reporting goes well beyond the financial statements as different types of flash reports (covered in Chapter 11) are produced daily, hourly, and even to the minute as heavily data-dependent businesses (e.g., retailers) can now, thanks to digital information and technology, literally monitor the effectiveness of a new advertising campaign within minutes of its being launched. Finally, we also would like to emphasize that strength in accuracy (refer to Chapter 5) is critical, as speed in reporting is dependent on highly accurate information.

5. Completeness: The concept of completeness really lies in the eye of the beholder, or rather is based on the specific needs of the target audience. For example, a general manager of a manufacturing plant will need a complete income statement for that plant, but not neces-sarily for the entire company. Further, the income statement should also include all relevant financial information, including prior-year comparisons, a budget-to-actual-variance analysis, key performance indicators (KPIs), and so on. Another example would be a sales team manager that is focused on top-line sales for a region through the gross profit or margin generated, which may be compared against the budget or even other regions' performances. If that party does not have bottom-line responsibility, then there is no need to provide a complete income statement.

 In a nutshell, internally produced financial informa-tion needs to be presented in a manner that assists your target audience with efficiently and effectively interpreting critical financial data and results. We can-not emphasize enough the importance of this func-tion, the ability for accountants and financial types to effectively communicate complex information to other professionals and management team members, which is often the Achilles heel of the so-called numbers people. Do the numbers people know debits, credits, GAAP, FASB, and how to communicate with external numbers people? Yes. But what really separates the best-in-class companies from the pack is having their numbers people be extremely strong communi-cators and educators as well.

A DEEPER DIVE AND EXAMPLE OF INTERNAL FINANCIAL INFORMATION

To assist readers, two additional examples of internal financial information have been provided in Exhibits 3.2 and 3.3.

EXHIBIT 3.2   Unaudited Operating Division Income Statement

Unaudited - Prepared by Company Management

QW Example Tech., Inc.
Unaudited Financial Statements
By Primary Division
For the Fiscal Year Ending
12/31/2020

Income Statement for the Fiscal Year Ending	Product Div. 12/31/2020	% of Net Rev.	Software Div. 12/31/2020	% of Net Rev.	
Revenue:					
Software Platform & SAAS Sales	$5,512,500	24.52%	$49,612,500	99.80%	Notice large discounts in the Product division. This division is dying with large discounts needed to move old products.
Product Sales	$19,679,625	87.52%	$401,625	0.81%	
Other Sales, Discounts, & Allowances	($2,707,200)	-12.04%	($300,800)	-0.61%	
Net Revenue	$22,484,925	100.00%	$49,713,325	100.00%	
Costs of Goods Sold:					
Direct Product Costs	$10,824,100	48.14%	$220,900	0.44%	
Wages & Burden, Software Sys. & SAAS Sales	$3,142,200	13.97%	$12,568,800	25.28%	
Direct Overhead	$665,000	2.96%	$35,000	0.07%	
Other Costs of Goods Sold	$21,250	0.09%	$63,750	0.13%	
Total Costs of Goods Sold	$14,652,550	65.17%	$12,888,450	25.93%	
Gross Profit	$7,832,375	34.83%	$36,824,875	74.07%	Software division has much higher gross margin and contribution margin as this represents the growth segment of the business. Old product business is struggling to breakeven.
Gross Margin		34.83%		74.07%	
Direct Operating Expenses:					
Advertising, Promotional, & Selling	$1,202,130	5.35%	$4,808,520	9.67%	
Personnel Wages, Burden, & Compensation	$1,168,738	5.20%	$3,506,213	7.05%	
Facility Operating Expenses	$4,032,000	17.93%	$2,268,000	4.56%	
Other Operating Expenses	$112,500	0.50%	$337,500	0.68%	
Total Direct Operating Expenses	$6,515,368	28.98%	$10,920,233	21.97%	
Contribution Profit	$1,317,008	5.86%	$25,904,643	52.11%	
Contribution Margin		5.86%		52.11%	

Confidential - Property of QW Example Tech., Inc.

Exhibit 3.2 breaks down the company's operations (through the contribution margin) between its two main operating divisions, product sales and software/SaaS sales. What is clear is that the product division is struggling and has been for years, as shown in Exhibit 3.1; product sales have declined on a year-over-year basis, whereas software sales have rocketed higher. Further, you can see that most sales discounts and allowances are centered in the product division (because of having to use aggressive discounts to move old products) and that the product division barely breaks even at the contribution income level. With this additional level of information, we can see in more detail that the company's business strategy associated with transitioning from a product-centric business to a software/SaaS model is starting to pay dividends in 2020 as both the top-line (increased from $53.7 million in 2019

EXHIBIT 3.3 Unaudited Company Sales Report by Primary Software /SaaS Product Line

Unaudited - Prepared by Company Management

QW Example Tech., Inc.
Unaudited Sales Analysis
For Software/SaaS
For the Fiscal Year Ending
12/31/2020

Sales by Product Type for the Fiscal Year Ending	Forecast 12/31/2020	% of Net Rev.	Actual 12/31/2020	% of Net Rev.	Variance	
Revenue:						
Software Installation Platform	$4,125,000	7.50%	$1,587,500	3.20%	($2,537,500)	Notice the negative variances with installation and expert and positive variance with basic.
SaaS Platform Basic	$11,000,000	20.00%	$12,250,000	24.69%	$1,250,000	
SaaS Platform Advanced	$22,000,000	40.00%	$21,800,000	43.94%	($200,000)	
SaaS Platform Expert	$16,500,000	30.00%	$12,750,000	25.70%	($3,750,000)	
Other Software Sales	$1,375,000	2.50%	$1,225,000	2.47%	($150,000)	
Total Sales Revenue	$55,000,000	100.00%	$49,612,500	100.00%	($5,387,500)	

Confidential - Property of QW Example Tech., Inc.

to $72.2 million in 2020) and the bottom-line (increased from a loss in 2019 of $248,000 to net profit of $2.9 million in 2020) growth have been impressive.

Another point of note with Exhibit 3.2 is that we have elected to cut off the presentation of the financial information at the contribution profit level. The reason for this is simple: This report is designed to focus management's attention on contributed earnings for each primary division (as the audience for the purposes of this report do not have control or authority over corporate overhead expenses).

Taking this analysis one step further, we would direct your attention to Exhibit 3.3, which represents a highly focused or specific sales flash report. The target audience for this report is the sales team that has management responsibility for software and SaaS sales. Exhibit 3.3 reports sales financial information for the entire year but it could just as easily report sales covering a monthly or quarterly period. As you can see in Exhibit 3.3, the total sales figure of $49.6 million agrees with the division income statement total sales figure of $49.6 million in Exhibit 3.2.

What you might notice in Exhibit 3.3 as that although the year-over-year sales revenue growth for the software division has been impressive, it has fallen short of the forecast. Even more interesting is that the main shortfall was centered in the SaaS Platform Expert product line, whereas a positive variance was realized in the SaaS Platform Basic product line. There could be any number of reasons for these variances, ranging from customer preference to the company not having the right resources dedicated to the selling cycle supporting the Expert product line but whatever the cause, this result warrants a deeper management review and analysis to implement corrective action.

Countless other examples of internally generated financial information and reports could be provided but no matter what information is generated, the same concept holds. Deliver the right information to the right party in the right format at the right time to support business decisions.

IN SUMMARY – DON'T MAKE THESE ROOKIE MISTAKES!

First, do not ever confuse internal financial information with external financial reporting. If it is not clear by now, these two have vastly different uses, purposes, and audiences.

Second, never just hit the Send button. Although tempting, any financial information distributed to external parties should always be reviewed and approved by all appropriate personnel and management.

 Third, a word of caution to aspiring entrepreneurs: Assumption is the mother of all you-know-whats; that is, if financial statements are requested, by internal or external parties (especially external), your policy should be loud and clear. The financial information is always reviewed, scrubbed, and so on by the appropriate company personnel before it is distributed. Do not assume that you can push a couple of buttons and print a report from accounting systems such as QuickBooks, Sage 50, or Net Suite, and then distribute this information. This can be a fatal mistake and almost always leads to far more questions and problems than it solves.

Fourth, all financial information distributed, whether to external parties or for internal use, should clearly note two key items. First is that the financial information is either audited or unaudited and second is that the financial information is confidential and the property of the company. Even for companies that have the best safeguards installed to protect their internal financial information, at some point this information is going to end up outside the organization, so it is always helpful (from a legal perspective) to have clear disclosures as to the confidential nature of the information.

CHAPTER 4

The Importance of Completeness

ESSENTIAL TO UNDERSTANDING THE BIG PICTURE

Let us start with a simple analogy. If a doctor completed an annual physical medical examination and only administered a limited number of tests and provided even fewer results, most people would find this unacceptable. What is needed (and expected) is a full examination with all results made available and, ideally, comparisons against key benchmarks for similar demographics (e.g., what should the cholesterol level be for a man my age?). The concept of completeness is no different for a business than a person, as to gain a full understanding of a company's operating results, potential risks, and opportunities, complete financial reporting is essential.

To better understand the concept of completeness, we provide examples of internal and external financial information reporting, starting with relatively weak or poor information through what at a minimum would be considered essential to successfully operate a business in today's challenging climate. For ease of presentation, our examples are focused on the big three financial statements (which we learned in previous chapters have a limited internal audience), but the concept holds for any internal financial information distributed.

The concept of completeness should always include presenting financial information against some type of benchmark or target, such as internally prepared forecasts, prior-year results, industry averages or standards, and so on. It should go without saying that it is one thing to present the financial results of a company, but without having something to measure these financial results against, gaining a full understanding of the company's operating results would basically be akin to going into surgery without knowing what you are trying to fix.

BARELY ACCEPTABLE (THE WORLD OF SMALL BUSINESSES)

We start our discussion with what would be considered the bare minimum in terms of providing financial information to either internal or external parties, that is, single-year financial statements that really boil down to providing just the current-year income statement and balance sheet (as the cash flow statement is not provided). For any serious business owner, investor, or manager, this bare minimum approach is not acceptable, but you would be absolutely amazed at how often companies can get by with providing such limited financial information. Even more amazing is how often external parties such as banks, investors, government agencies, and the like are willing to accept this limited level of information for analysis purposes and then to base a decision upon it. Whatever the reason or logic, Exhibit 4.1 presents what would be considered the bare minimum when providing a balance sheet and Exhibit 4.2 an income statement.

Taking a closer look at the financial statements presented in Exhibits 4.1 and 4.2, the following should jump out at you:

> ➢ Our sample company is a small professional services business operating out of a single office in a large city. Like most smaller companies, audited or reviewed financial statements are not available, as these types of businesses generally rely heavily on internally prepared financial information. Further, you will almost never see footnotes attached to internally generated financial statements.

> ➢ Notice the different reporting format used for the income statement Exhibit 4.2 compared to Exhibit 1.1. It not only provides too much detail (as some of the expenses should probably be grouped together when reported) but, in addition, it uses a standard reporting technique

EXHIBIT 4.1 Example Small Company Unaudited Balance Sheet

Unaudited - Prepared by Company Management

Local Sample Service Co, Inc.
Unaudited Financial Statements
For the Fiscal Year Ending
12/31/2020

Balance Sheet Period Ending	FYE 12/31/2020
Current Assets:	
Cash Accounts, Operating, Payroll & MM	$284,521
Accounts Receivable, Net	$531,453
Prepaid Expenses	$42,100
Total Current Assets	$858,074
Long-Term Operating & Other Assets:	
Office Equipment, Furniture, & Computers	$178,250
Company Vehicles	$135,000
Accumulated Depreciation	($147,500)
Net Fixed Assets	$165,750
Other Assets:	
Other Assets & Deposits	$15,000
Total Long-Term Operating & Other Assets	$180,750
Total Assets	**$1,038,824**

No prior year information is provided. Also, note the added descriptions offered with the cash accounts, a common presentation format with smaller companies.

Added information provided related to company assets including reference to vehicles.

Balance Sheet Period Ending Liabilities	12/31/2020
Current Liabilities:	
Accounts & Professional Fees Payable	$42,200
Accrued Payroll & Compensation	$68,412
Line of Credit, Outstanding Balance	$106,291
Other Current Liabilities & Customer Deposits	$18,875
Total Current Liabilities	$235,778
Long-term Liabilities:	
Note Payable Bank, Vehicles	$75,000
Total Liabilities	**$310,778**
Owners' Equity	
Common Stock	$150,000
Distributions of Earnings	($777,089)
Retained Earnings	$1,055,105
Current Year Net Income (Loss)	$300,030
Total Stockholders' Equity	**$728,047**
Total Liabilities & Stockholders' Equity	**$1,038,824**

Again, added detail provided with account descriptions as small companies generally lack sophistication when presenting financial information.

Usually a much more simplistic capital table with only common equity, distributions of earnings, retained earnings, and current year income (loss).

Confidential - Property of Local Sample Service Co, Inc.

that lists all expenses in alpha order (that is common when preparing income tax returns). Note: We presented this reporting format not only to highlight the fact that small businesses often utilize this type of reporting but, in addition, to emphasize that while this reporting format may be accurate, it doesn't present information in a reliable manner (refer to Chapter 6).

EXHIBIT 4.2 Example Small Company Unaudited Income Statement

Unaudited - Prepared by Company Management

Local Sample Service Co, Inc.
Unaudited Financial Statements
For the Fiscal Year Ending
12/31/2020

Income Statement Period Ending	FYE 12/31/2020
Sales Revenue:	
Professional Fees Billed	$3,955,000
Direct Expense Reimbursement	$296,625
Total Sales Revenue	$4,251,625
Costs of Sales:	
Personnel Wages & Burden	$1,381,778
Subcontractors & Consultants	$850,325
Third Party Fees Incurred	$393,275
Total Costs of Sales	$2,625,378
Gross Profit	$1,626,247
Selling, Operating, & Administrative Expenses:	
Advertising	$78,450
Dues & Subscriptions	$25,680
Insurance, General	$42,500
Insurance, Health, Life, & Disability	$42,000
Marketing & Promotional	$30,000
Office Expenses & Supplies	$20,525
Payroll	$497,500
Payroll Taxes	$47,263
Professional Fees, Legal & Acctg.	$27,500
Rent	$260,013
Telecommunications	$18,750
Travel, Lodging, Meals, & Entertainment	$124,500
Utilities	$37,702
Website Maintenance	$18,000
Total Selling, Operating, & Admin. Expenses	$1,270,382
Operating Profit	$355,864
Other Expenses:	
Charitable Contributions	$5,000
Depreciation Expense	$39,156
Interest Expense	$10,877
Income Tax Expense	$800
Total Other Expenses	$55,834
Net Income (Loss)	$300,030

Confidential - Property of Local Sample Service Co, Inc.

This company has elected to provide additional levels of detail in the income statement as they are using the financial statement for both internal and external presentation purposes.

Notice a number of items including the level of detail (indicates inexperienced team releasing the income statement), all expenses listed in alpha order (simple order used for tax reporting), and some rather large expenses (travel fairly high, most likely owners running through auto expenses).

Income tax expense lumped in with other as this entity uses a tax passthrough structure as is formed as a Sub-Chapter S corporation.

➢ The lack of information, including not providing comparable prior-year results, not including a statement of cash flows, and offering no ratio analysis, indicates that the company's internal accounting and financial management resources may be limited. This format does not help the reader understand much other than the basics.

> You may also note that this company has only $800 of income tax expense compared to taxable income of over $400,000. How is this possible? The answer lies in the fact that this entity is structured as a Subchapter S corporation, which means that all taxable profits and losses are passed through to the individual owners of the company (who are then responsible for remitting income taxes on the profits passed through at the personal level). Also, you will note the reference to distributions of earnings in the owners' equity section of the balance sheet as opposed to the company issuing dividends. In tax pass-through entities, distributions of earnings are made (and not dividends) to return excess profits to the owners that are commonly used to cover personal income tax obligations (from the pass-through of profits).

Needless to say, the financial statements presented in Exhibits 4.1 and 4.2 are nowhere near being best in class, so you may ask why we went to the trouble. Well, the answer is simple. Based on the latest data available for October 2020, there are approximately 17.6 million businesses operating in the United States, of which almost 90% generate less than $10 million a year in sales revenue and have less than 100 employees. And the financial reporting norm for much of the 90% business group will most likely be something akin to Exhibits 4.1 and 4.2, so for any party that spends a fair amount of time dealing with small businesses, this reporting format will most likely be the norm.

BETTER AND APPROPRIATE FOR THE EXTERNAL AUDIENCE

Progressing up the food chain to the next tranche of businesses, that is, the 10% that are much larger and more sophisticated, we direct your attention back to Chapter 1 and refer to Exhibits 1.1, 1.2, and 1.3. We are not going to re-present these exhibits but will emphasize that the next leg up when presenting complete financial statements includes the following:

> The financial statements will have a much higher likelihood of being audited or, at a minimum, reviewed (by external CPA firms) and should include financial statement footnotes (covered in Chapter 2); translation, the financial information is more reliable.
> The financial statements will be presented in a more technical accounting structure in a format adhering to GAAP. This compares

to financial information prepared for internal evaluation and use that may not always be in accordance with GAAP.

➢ For public companies and extremely large private companies, full financial reports should also be available. The additional financial reports will most likely include an overview of the company's financial performance, key milestones met, benchmark comparisons, and other selected results (to help educate or, should we say, sway the external audience).

➢ Comparable and complete financial information is provided, as multiple years of data should be presented along with ensuring that the statement of cash flows is included.

This middle-of-the-road level of completeness is the minimum or standard level expected for distribution to external parties by both public companies and larger, private businesses – that is, full disclosure as required by GAAP with select additional information provided but always, and I mean always, with the understanding that this financial information is targeted for use by external parties (and available publicly). You will note that we make the reference to larger, private businesses using this standard external reporting structure in a similar fashion to publicly traded companies. While there is no legal requirement that larger, private companies use this reporting structure, most do, as external parties, including investors, lenders, banks, and so on, will demand the same information. Their logic is simple: When the stakes are raised (i.e., significantly higher loans and investments being made), the level and quality of financial information distributed is also raised.

LET'S TAKE IT UP A NOTCH TO BEST IN CLASS

Finally, our discussion on completeness will evolve to a level designed for use primarily by internal company management team members. We are going to present just the income statement (in Exhibit 4.3) to avoid overkill, but it should be noted that the type of completeness disclosed in Exhibit 4.3 can similarly be applied to the balance sheet and statement of cash flows, as well as countless other internal financial reports and information prepared for a company's management team. For anyone interested, Exhibits 4.4 and 4.5 (which cover the balance sheet and statement of cash flows) are available in the Excel workbook file, which you can request and will be sent to you free of charge.

Okay, there is a hell of a lot more financial and even operational information presented that is significantly more robust than what was provided to the external users. As we dig in deeper to the financial information presented in Exhibit 4.3, we call your attention to the following items:

➤ The financial statement variance analysis presented in Exhibit 4.3 is designed for internal use only and for select executive management. The financial information, while consistent with the externally audited financial statements (as the net income for 2020 is the exact same at $2.914 million), is confidential and has not been audited (but rather prepared internally).

➤ Prior-year operating comparisons are helpful (which we have done with 2019 and 2020), but comparing actual results to forecast results is usually much better. The goal with most companies is to reach or exceed the financial performance targets established in the business plan and forecasts, so this is where management tends to focus their attention (i.e., what went right and what went wrong).

➤ We have included a select few key performance indicators (KPIs) in the financial analysis as, for the target internal audience, the KPIs selected are critical to understanding the business performance. There are countless KPIs that could be incorporated into the financial analysis but those included should be critical to quickly and efficiently understanding the company's performance.

➤ Far more information and detail has been provided, which generally requires additional management attention, analysis, and support to verify. Although it was not provided in Exhibit 4.3 (because of space limitations), a management overview and explanation of the positive and negative variances should be attached. For example, a negative sales variance of $5.1 million was realized between actual 2020 results and forecast 2020 results. As shown in the exhibit, the company exceeded its target number of SaaS customers by 25 (forecast of 500 compared to actual of 525). So, what's the problem? Well, customers ended up purchasing a higher number of Basic SaaS software products compared to the Expert SaaS software platform (at a lower price point). Management will certainly want to understand this customer preference and how to better prepare in the coming years.

➤ You will notice the three highlighted areas, which at a macro level are the root cause of why the company "missed" its forecasted operating results. First, sales came in below forecasts by roughly 6.5% or $5.1 million (which was explained in the previous bullet point). Second, other

EXHIBIT 4.3 Unaudited Company Income Statement Variance & KPI Analysis

Unaudited - Prepared by Company Management

QW Example Tech., Inc.
Unaudited Financial Statements
& Variance Analysis
For the Fiscal Year Ending
12/31/2020

Income Statement for the Fiscal Year Ending	Actual 12/31/2019	% of Net Rev.	Actual 12/31/2020	% of Net Rev.	Forecast 12/31/2020	% of Net Rev.	Variance
Key Performance Indicators:							
Revenue per Full-Time Employee	$537,470		$591,789		$618,400		($26,611)
Product Sales, Avg. Order Value (net)	$29,663		$24,390		$26,400		($2,010)
Software Platform & SAAS Sales:							
SAAS Sales, Total Customer Accounts	400		525		500		25
SAAS Sales, Total Earned Avg. per Account	$70,875		$89,143		$99,000		($9,857)
Revenue:							
Software Platform & SAAS Sales	$31,500,000	58.61%	$55,125,000	76.35%	$57,500,000	74.39%	($2,375,000)
Product Sales	$23,625,000	43.96%	$20,081,250	27.81%	$22,000,000	28.46%	($1,918,750)
Other Sales, Discounts, & Allowances	($1,378,000)	-2.56%	($3,008,000)	-4.17%	($2,200,000)	-2.85%	($808,000)
Net Revenue	$53,747,000	100.00%	$72,198,250	100.00%	$77,300,000	100.00%	($5,101,750)
Costs of Goods Sold:							
Direct Product Costs	$12,994,000	24.18%	$11,045,000	15.30%	$11,000,000	14.23%	($45,000)
Wages & Burden	$10,395,000	19.34%	$15,711,000	21.76%	$15,575,000	20.15%	($136,000)
Direct Overhead	$800,000	1.49%	$700,000	0.97%	$750,000	0.97%	$50,000
Other Costs of Goods Sold	$70,000	0.13%	$85,000	0.12%	$100,000	0.13%	$15,000

Total Costs of Goods Sold	$24,259,000	45.14%	$27,541,000	38.15%	$27,425,000	35.48%	($116,000)
Gross Profit	$29,488,000	54.86%	$44,657,250	61.85%	$49,875,000	64.52%	($5,217,750)
Gross Margin	54.86%		61.85%		64.52%		n/a
Direct Operating Expenses:							
Advertising, Promotional, & Selling	$4,232,700	7.88%	$6,010,650	8.33%	$6,000,000	7.76%	($10,650)
Personnel Wages, Burden, & Compensation	$3,056,950	5.69%	$4,674,950	6.48%	$5,000,000	6.47%	$325,050
Facility Operating Expenses	$5,250,000	9.77%	$6,300,000	8.73%	$6,000,000	7.76%	($300,000)
Other Operating Expenses	$375,000	0.70%	$450,000	0.62%	$500,000	0.65%	$50,000
Total Direct Operating Expenses	$12,914,650	24.03%	$17,435,600	24.15%	$17,500,000	22.64%	$64,400
Contribution Profit	$16,573,350	30.84%	$27,221,650	37.70%	$32,375,000	41.88%	($5,153,350)
Contribution Margin	30.84%		37.70%		41.88%		n/a
Corporate Expenses & Overhead:							
Corporate Marketing, Branding, & Promotional	$2,116,350	3.94%	$2,671,400	3.70%	$2,500,000	3.23%	($171,400)
Research, Development, & Design	$10,749,000	20.00%	$12,996,000	18.00%	$13,527,500	17.50%	$531,500
Corporate Overhead & Support	$1,875,000	3.49%	$2,250,000	3.12%	$2,500,000	3.23%	$250,000
Depreciation & Amortization Expense	$1,814,286	3.38%	$2,421,429	3.35%	$2,400,000	3.10%	($21,429)
Total Operating Expenses	$16,554,636	30.80%	$20,338,829	28.17%	$20,927,500	27.07%	$588,671
Operating Income (EBIT)	$18,714	0.03%	$6,882,821	9.53%	$11,447,500	14.81%	($4,564,679)
Operating Margin (EBIT Margin)	0.03%		9.53%		14.81%		n/a

(Continued)

EXHIBIT 4.3   (Continued)

Unaudited - Prepared by Company Management

QW Example Tech., Inc.
Unaudited Financial Statements
& Variance Analysis
For the Fiscal Year Ending
12/31/2020

Income Statement for the Fiscal Year Ending	Actual 12/31/2019	% of Net Rev.	Actual 12/31/2020	% of Net Rev.	Forecast 12/31/2020	% of Net Rev.	Variance
Other Expenses (Income):							
Other Expenses, Income, & Discontinued Ops.	$250,000	0.47%	$2,000,000	2.77%	$500,000	0.65%	($1,500,000)
Interest Expense	$150,000	0.28%	$400,000	0.55%	$425,000	0.55%	$25,000
Total Other Expenses (Income)	$400,000	0.74%	$2,400,000	3.32%	$925,000	1.20%	($1,475,000)
Net Income (Loss) Before Taxes	($381,286)	-0.71%	$4,482,821	6.21%	$10,522,500	13.61%	($6,039,679)
Income Tax Expense (Benefit)	($133,000)	-0.25%	$1,569,000	2.17%	$3,682,875	4.76%	$2,113,875
Net Income (Loss) After Taxes	($248,286)	-0.46%	$2,913,821	4.04%	$6,839,625	8.85%	($3,925,804)

Confidential - Property of QW Example Tech., Inc.

expenses of $2 million were realized compared to a forecast level of $500,000. Third, income tax expense was well below the forecasts, which should be easy to understand as with lower profits come lower income taxes. But the intriguing question is why the company realized a negative $1.5 million variance in other expenses. This will be fully disclosed as we move through the remainder of the book.

 We do want to pass along one additional key concept, as it relates to the distribution of this level of financial information. In certain cases, critical external parties such as strategic partners or large capital sources may be provided access to this financial information as it can help build credibility and confidence with these partners, knowing that management is on top of their financial and accounting game.

COMPLETENESS REVISITED

Preparing complete financial information represents an integral part of developing and maintaining best-in-class financial reporting systems, for both internal management review and business decision-making and external analysis. Completeness is a broad subject that is heavily influenced by the financial information reporting needs of the target audience. But remember that *completeness* represents just the first letter in *CART*, as without *accurate*, *reliable*, and *timely* financial information, the effectiveness of providing complete financial information is often muted.

Also note that providing complete financial information does not magically originate from business "day one" as companies will need to develop, over time, their financial information reporting systems to find that ideal and reliable format, with just the proper balance of detail versus summary information, all packaged and delivered in a timely manner. Operating a business in today's economic environment requires a keen focus on ensuring that complete financial information is available on which to adjust business plans on the turn of a dime.

CHAPTER 5

Accuracy versus Reliability, Not to Be Confused

DO NOT CONFUSE THESE TWO CRITICAL AND INTERCONNECTED CONCEPTS

In Chapter 4, we touched on the importance of producing complete financial information as a critical component to the business evaluation and decision-making process. What is important to remember about producing complete financial information is that it is 100% dependent on a properly functioning accounting information system that produces both accurate and reliable financial information. Or, stated differently, you cannot prepare complete financial information without having the assurance that your accounting system generates both accurate and reliable information.

As we dive further into our discussion on this topic, let's first provide definitions for both accuracy and reliability, starting with *Webster's Dictionary* and then expanding on the definitions within the context of an accounting environment.

➢ Accuracy: *Webster's Dictionary* defines *accuracy* as "freedom from mistake or error" and further "conformity to a truth or to a standard or model." This is an excellent starting point, but to expand on this from an accounting perspective, the reference to "freedom from mistake or

51

error" needs to be understood, keeping in mind the all-important concept of materiality (discussed later in this chapter). In my travels of 35+ years, I have never seen an accounting and financial reporting system produce 100% accurate information, as there is always some number of small differences, mistakes, rounding errors, and so on. The key with an accounting system producing accurate information is that "material" errors, mistakes, omissions, and so on are avoided or eliminated with a tolerance level established for minor mistakes or errors (that do not distort the financial information produced by a business).

➢ Reliability (i.e., reliable): Again, we turn to *Webster's Dictionary*, which defines being reliable as "suitable or fit to be relied upon" and further, "giving the same result on successive trials." This makes perfect sense as the goal with producing reliable financial information is to enable a company's management team to rely on this information on which to make sound economic and business decisions (in a consistent manner, regardless of number of analyses completed). Further, what will become clear in our discussion on producing reliable financial information is how critically important it is to properly format, structure, and present this information so that a company's management team can efficiently understand the information, draw effective conclusions, and make important business decisions (in a timely and assured manner).

We provide examples in Chapter 6 of just how important preparing reliable financial statements and information is, but first we have no choice but to cover a topic that I know is near and dear to everyone's heart (yes, heavy sarcasm) – accounting!

A CRASH COURSE IN ACCOUNTING

We know, it's hard to believe that a bunch of accountants would want to spend some of your valuable time talking about accounting concepts and theories. Yes, we agree that this topic is generally best left to a bunch of bean counters who live and breathe debits and credits. In fact, most readers of this book might take this opportunity to peruse this portion of the chapter when they are having trouble falling asleep at night (as reading this material will certainly do the trick). However, before you doze off and if you elect to remember anything about our brief, albeit extremely important, conversation on accounting, it would be these two thoughts:

1. Accounting is the function responsible for producing basically all financial information, data, reports, statements, and so on (herein and throughout the book referred to as financial information). Or, put differently, the accounting system is the primary source of generating critical business financial data.

2. Finance is the function responsible for analyzing, evaluating, and assessing the accounting data on which business and economic decisions are based. To keep this thought even simpler, remember the acronym GIGO (garbage in, garbage out). It should be readily apparent now just how important the accounting function is, as if the accounting system is producing garbage data, there is no way sound business and economic decisions can be made.

Most everyone would agree that both accounting and finance represent critical business functions and often overlap and/or are "joined at the hip," but they differ from an input/output perspective, as accounting is, for lack of a better term, the start of the food chain (as it relates to generating financial information) and finance tends to be the end of the food chain (as it relates to analyzing financial information).

So now that we have your attention, we attempt to provide a crash course in accounting principles and theory in less than half a chapter. Our goal is not to provide a detailed overview of accounting rules or guidelines such as the theory behind accounting for capital asset leases or applying Black-Scholes to account for stock option expense, but rather to offer a 10,000-foot overview of accounting and key concepts every business must address, starting with this fundamental statement:

To produce accurate financial information, every business must develop, implement, maintain, and manage a properly functioning accounting system that at its foundation relies on establishing, implementing, and adhering to agreed-upon accounting policies, procedures, and controls applied on a consistent basis and in accordance with GAAP.

And what does GAAP stand for? Generally Accepted Accounting Principles, whose simplest definition is "a set of rules that encompass the details, complexities, and legalities of business and corporate accounting." These rules are established by various accounting organizations, boards, and groups, with the primary group being the Financial Accounting Standards Board (FASB), which uses GAAP as the foundation for its comprehensive set of approved accounting methods and practices.

There you have it – when producing financial information, businesses should adhere to GAAP as established by FASB. Seems simple enough, but as you work through this chapter it should become abundantly clear that GAAP is more or less a series of guidelines businesses can use that provide a certain amount of leeway when actual financial information is produced. Or maybe the best way to think of it is referring to this quote from Captain Barbosa from the *Pirates of the Caribbean* franchise: "And thirdly, the code (translation to accounting – GAAP) is more what you'd call *guidelines* than actual *rules*." With this said, let us expand on your understanding of GAAP by providing a summary of various macro-level accounting concepts that help provide certain guardrails for businesses when producing financial information.

KEY ACCOUNTING THEORIES, CONCEPTS, AND TRENDS

One thing that we are not going to do is get into a detailed discussion on understanding accounting concepts, rules, and principles (from a technical perspective). If you genuinely want to understand accounting in more depth, please refer to a book my father wrote, *Accounting for Dummies*, which provides an excellent introduction into the basics of accounting. Further, it would be pointless in the span of one chapter (or for that matter, in one book) to try and explain the concepts that dance around in an accountant's head each day. Even I, myself, being an accountant, would simply rather be put out of my misery than spending hours upon hours deciphering all the technical concepts and guidelines accountants follow when producing financial statements, reports, and information.

Rather, what we have elected to do is summarize macro-level accounting theories, concepts, and current trends to help you gain a better understand of how financial information is prepared and what overlying broad governances and, yes, politics, come into play when preparing financial information.

- Art versus science: Probably the single most important concept to understand with accounting is that it really is more of an art than a science. Accounting rules and guidelines are not set in stone or laid out in black-and-white terms. Rather, accounting includes a fair amount of subjectivity when it comes to producing financial information (as you will see shortly) and relies just as much on qualitative factors as quantitative analyses.

➤ Internal Pressure and Politics: It must be noted that accounting is a profession that is not immune from politics and internal reporting pressures. You can be assured that there have been many lively internal discussions between the executive management team members or C-suite (i.e., chief-level positions, including the CEO, COO, CFO, etc.), the board of directors, and the finance and accounting groups as to finalizing periodic financial statements and reports to ensure that the company "hits the numbers." Please note that we are not saying that companies are committing fraud to achieve certain financial operating results but rather a more subtle approach may be used to change an estimate here or adjust an analysis there to squeeze a few more dollars out of the financial results.

➤ Accrual versus cash (or other basis): Simply put, accrual-based accounting measures a company's performance, position, or results by recognizing economic events regardless of when cash transactions occur. This is the essence of GAAP. For example, in the income statement, revenue is recognized when it is earned (as opposed to collecting cash) and expenses are realized expenses when they are incurred (as opposed to when cash is disbursed).

Almost every business professional, at one time or another, has heard reference made to financial statements being prepared on an accrual versus a cash basis. While cash basis reporting is allowed in certain circumstances (e.g., for reporting taxable income to the IRS), it should be noted that no serious business utilizes the cash basis of reporting for external reporting to capital sources or to make important business and economic decisions. For almost all businesses (and to be taken seriously), GAAP must be adhered to and implemented. Period!

➤ The matching principle: This concept is relatively straightforward and best understood by referring to an example from the income statement. Under the matching principle, earned revenues should be matched against appropriate expenses during a given period. For example, if a company recognizes earned revenue of $1 million over a monthly reporting period, any sales commissions that are owed to a sales representative should be expensed in the same period, regardless of when the commissions are paid. Another perfect example relates to Tesla. When Tesla records sales of vehicles, it must also estimate and record an appropriate expense for future warranty claims (as Tesla provides a multiyear warranty for product defects on new auto sales), even though it may be years before the warranty claims are presented and paid by the company.

➤ Conservative by nature: By being conservative we mean that accounting principles tend to be structured to realize expenses earlier and not recognize revenue/sales until the entire earnings process is complete (see below). Maybe being conservative is not all that fair but maybe it is just smart planning, as the accounting governance organizations realize that companies tend to be more aggressive with presenting results (so building in a conservative bias helps provide some balance). Of course, there are always exceptions to this rule, as anyone familiar with the epic failures at Enron will attest.

➤ Policies, procedures, and controls: The foundation of accuracy is centered in properly functioning accounting policies, procedures, and controls, administered by qualified professionals, adhering to GAAP, and applied on a consistent basis. This represents the bedrock of any sound accounting system and incorporates these critical components:

- Qualified staff: An experienced, qualified, committed, ethical, and diverse accounting staff that is respected by management and supported by the board of directors is a necessity. In addition, two essential traits are best summarized by Duke, played by Jack Palance in the movie *City Slickers II*, when explaining that "one thing is" honesty, integrity – two traits of utmost importance.

- Segregation of duties: Accounting and financial functions are intentionally segregated between different staff to protect company assets and produce CART financial information. We are sure everyone has heard the story of the reliable nice old lady who has been the company's bookkeeper for 20+ years only to realize she has bilked the company out of hundreds of thousands of dollars over the years. What better parties are there at committing and hiding fraud than the top accounting and financial staff, as they know exactly how to hide the dirt and conceal the truth? Therefore, it is always recommended that while it's fine to have the accounting or finance department review, account for, and authorize payments, the movement of cash and final approval of the payments should come from a segregated department.

- Materiality: All businesses must evaluate and manage the trade-off between accounting for every dollar (flowing in and out of a company) and the cost of implementing this effort. This represents the heart of the materiality concept, as it is literally impossible for companies like Amazon or McDonald's to assure 100% accuracy with all financial transactions. Companies will establish accounting policies, procedures, and controls to ensure that no material misstatements are present in the financial information produced (but are willing to accept a small tolerance for errors if they are not significant). But remember, different parties have different perspectives on what exactly is "material," so be aware of this concept.

- Use of estimates: Basically, every operating business of size, in one fashion or another, will use estimates when preparing financial information. Businesses can range from a large, mature retailer that must record estimated returns and refunds after holiday selling season to a newer company such as Tesla that must estimate potential future warranty claims as a cost today against the sale. But similar to the concept of materiality, the use of estimates can be a sign or flag of potential accounting issues or misstatements. As a rule of thumb, the more a company must rely on the use of estimates to prepare financial statements or the newer or greener a company is (without having years of data available to properly analyze), the higher the chance an error may occur in the financial information prepared.

- Disclosing accounting changes: Speaking of estimates, companies will often update or revise estimates as additional data becomes available. This represents a perfectly normal process (if it is kept within reason). In addition, companies may also change an accounting policy to improve the accuracy of their financial reporting. Again, this happens from time to time and is not out of the ordinary. What does become a problem is when companies change estimates or accounting policies on a suspiciously frequent basis and, worse yet, do not properly disclose or communicate these changes (i.e., they bury the decision deep in the financial report somewhere). Lack of timely and clear disclosure of accounting changes is definitely a red flag.

➢ Current trends: Accounting and GAAP represent constantly evolving principles or functions that must adapt to changing economic and market conditions. This has been the case for the past 100 years and will undoubtedly be the case moving forward. Today is no different, as highlighted by the following three examples of current trends or hot topics:

• The earnings process: Revenue recognition is an extremely important and hot issue in today's economic environment – and rightfully so, as companies are always looking to drive top-line sales and display high rates of growth to justify nosebleed valuations. This issue really boils down to one key question that is much easier asked than answered: When is the earnings process complete? Or stated differently, when can a customer sale be recorded as earned revenue based on the company's operating model? Ask five different accountants and five different executives and you may get 10 different interpretations; that is how divisive this topic can be.

   For example, a technology company that sells an annual software subscription may take a position that 50% of the annual subscription should be recognized as earned revenue in the first three months, as this is when the customers need the most support (from internal staff to implement) and tend to use the software more frequently. An accountant, seeing that the term of the subscription is for one year, may say that only 25% of the subscription can be recognized as earned revenue in the first three months. Let the discussions and debates begin as in reality, it may be somewhere between (to ensure that expenses are matched against revenue). GAAP has provided guidelines to help determine when revenue can be recognized, but remember, accounting is just as much an art form as a science. We are not going to get into the details on GAAP revenue recognition but if you remember one thing it should be this – revenue recognition is often an area that is abused by companies (looking to improve operating results) and is almost always a heavy area of focus by CPA firms when conducting audits.

- Balance sheet comparability: For years, external parties have struggled with comparing balance sheets of two like companies operating in similar markets or industries. The reason for this is differences in how debt is disclosed and how companies may utilize "off-balance-sheet" debt to finance operations. A perfect example of this is the use of leases (or perceived rental agreements) compared to loans. A lease for equipment or real property, if properly structured, will generally not appear as debt on a company's balance sheet; rather, the periodic payment is recorded as rent or lease expense in the income statement. A similar company that secured a loan to buy the equipment (rather than lease it) will record the equipment as an asset, recognize the loan as debt, and then depreciate the equipment and realize interest expense on the loan. Same equipment, similar businesses, yet the balance sheets of the two companies will look different (and not be comparable).

  Off-balance-sheet transactions such as leases, special-purpose entities, and other clever financing vehicles have been used and abused for years, so the various accounting authoritative groups, including FASB, have sharpened their focus on this topic and are requiring companies to tighten up financial statement reporting to ensure that all debt and equivalents are properly presented and disclosed. There is no question that the trend is now squarely in the court of complete and full disclosure of all debt instruments.

- Company equity transactions: Companies will often use equity incentive plans to reward employees with additional compensation that is tied to the improved performance of a company's stock (or similar equity). This is a common practice with technology companies, as lucrative employee stock option grants are often made to key employees that can turn out being worth hundreds of thousands, if not millions, of dollars. The accounting industry recognized this issue and after much debate, evaluation, and discussion now requires companies to report employee stock option expense in their financial statements (based on approved models and formulas that calculate the expense).

  Additional examples could be provided that explain how companies leverage their own equity to support their business plan and finance operations, but the key trend to remember is that if a company's equity is going to be used in a financially meaningful manner, then the transaction(s) will need to be properly reported and disclosed in the financial statements and reports prepared. The concepts of comparability, matching, and disclosure all hold here as, again, two companies may utilize different strategies to finance operations and incentivize employees but need to be evaluated on a level playing field.

By now we are guessing that you have had more than your fill of accounting, so we will end our discussion at this point. But please remember that the very foundation of preparing best-in-class financial information starts with accuracy, all of which originates in a properly and efficiently functioning accounting system.

ROUNDING OUT OUR DISCUSSION

We would be remiss in our discussion on accuracy and accounting without providing some final thoughts, tips, and tidbits on the always-relevant topic of accounting and financial reporting fraud. Names such as Enron, Madoff, and, more recently, Wirecard should quickly come to mind as these represent high-profile frauds that resulted in billions of dollars of losses. But fraud is certainly not limited to billion-dollar companies, as it occurs at every level of business in almost every type of operating environment. So here are some thoughts on fraud that you may want to remember along the way.

First, it is important to understand the difference between financial errors and irregularities. Errors basically equate to an unintentional mistake that might be centered in a poor analysis, inexperienced staff, lack of proper reviews being completed, and so on. Irregularities represent an intentional effort to mislead or make a material misstatement with the willful intent to deceive or defraud.

Second, errors are more prone to occur in companies that are under-staffed, lack proper segregation of duties, do not utilize external parties (e.g., a CPA firm completing an audit) to validate financial information, have poorly functioning accounting systems, and so on. It should be noted that the financial damage inflicted from errors may be as great as from irregularities, as businesses that do not take the accounting function seriously can quickly experience significant pain.

Third, when management collusion is present, it is almost impossible for external parties to detect fraud over the short term. By management collusion we mean when the senior or executive management team is conspiring or colluding to mislead external parties or misstate financial information – good luck figuring this out before the company implodes.

 Fourth, periods of irrational exuberance (coined by former chairman of the Federal Reserve Board Alan Greenspan) tend to lead to more wild business claims, success stories, growth trajectories, and valuations, which can feed the fraud beast. When money's flowing freely, it seems that accounting is not a priority or is placed on the back burner. However, when business and market conditions turn, fraud starts to emerge and flow to the top of the pond (and stinks). Remember, the cash flow statement can help ferret out fraud, as it reports how a company generates and consumes cash and just how reliant a company may be on external financial sources (which tend to evaporate during financial crises).

Fifth and finally, the smartest and most cunning fraudsters seem to always be one step ahead of GAAP and the accounting industry. Eventually, fraud catches up with most everyone, but the crafty and clever parties seem to be able to get in front of it and push accounting to the limits (and seem to exit before all hell breaks loose, leaving someone else holding the bag).

In closing, we would like to emphasize that fraudulent financial information is the exception rather than the rule, as most companies make a concerted effort to produce CART financial information. However, in cases or situations where there are enough red flags to take pause and a step back, ask yourself these two questions: "Does it sound too good to be true?" and "Am I being sold or educated with the financial information?" If the answer is yes and sold, then you want to abide by the advice provided by one of the greatest investors of all time, Warren Buffett, who so diligently noted about expectations, "Honesty is a very expensive gift. Do not expect it from cheap people." What you will generally find when fraud is involved is that cheap people (i.e., without morals and ethics) are also present.

CHAPTER 6

Reliability and Timeliness, the Best of Friends

PRODUCING RELIABLE FINANCIAL INFORMATION

To close the discussion on the "what" and "when" of producing CART financial information, we will turn our discussion to the remaining two components – reliability and timeliness. What should be remembered with these two concepts is that for financial information to be reliable, it not only must be presented in the proper format and structure but, in addition, needs to be provided in the ideal time frame with the assurance of accuracy. Managing businesses in today's hyper-data-driven economy no longer affords companies the opportunity to delay producing and distributing financial information, as management cannot wait on critical data. Rather, management must be provided certain financial information in real time to assess operating results and, if needed, implement corrective business actions.

The second section of this chapter focuses on the timeliness of financial information reporting, both as dictated by external parties and required by internal management, but we start by diving into the topic of financial information reliability and direct you to Exhibit 4.2 presented in Chapter 4. This exhibit provides a crash course in understanding the importance and difference between accuracy and reliability.

Exhibit 4.2 presents the income statement of a small professional service company that realized approximately $4.25 million a year in sales revenue for 2020, resulting in a net profit of approximately $300,000. Okay, this seems reasonable as generating a profit of roughly 7% on sales revenue is probably not out of the ordinary and it is assumed that the accuracy of the information is sound. As previously discussed, Exhibit 4.2 offers a look at a standard reporting format used by small businesses for income statements that displays sales revenue first, costs of goods second, and then provides a detailed listing of operating expenses followed by disclosing other expenses. While this format of an income statement is widely used (by small businesses), it will drive home the key concept of accuracy versus reliability.

Exhibit 6.1 takes the income statement presented in Exhibit 4.2 and reformats the information into a more useful and easier-to-understand layout. As you can see, 2020 was not kind to this company when compared to 2019, but as you work through financial information presented, it will become evident as to why the year-over-year performance was so poor. Items of interest and focus are the following:

➢ The income statement presented in Exhibit 4.2 was structured using a descriptive format with expense accounts listed in alphabetical order (and providing too much detail). Exhibit 6.1 presents the income statement using a functional format that groups or combines like expenses to help third parties understand relationships and ratios more efficiently (removing excess detail and confidential information).

➢ Completeness is on full display with the income statement presented in Exhibit 6.1 as not only is the prior-year information presented, but analytical analyses have been included, such as calling out employee KPIs and even capturing balance sheet data. One item we would draw your attention to is the distribution of earnings analysis. As can be seen from Exhibit 6.1, the $777,000 of earnings distributions is reasonable (at 50%) compared to the prior-year net profit of $1.554 million. Distribution of earnings on a delayed or lagged basis is common with smaller companies, as they often defer distributions for three to six months after the previous fiscal year-end (to finalize the financial results and individual income tax obligations). If you were to simply evaluate the distributions of earnings against the current-year net profit of $300,000, you might think the company was crazy to distribute so much cash in excess of profitability.

EXHIBIT 6.1   Example Small Company Unaudited Comparable Income Statements and KPIs

Unaudited - Prepared by Company Management

Local Sample Service Co, Inc.
Unaudited Financial Statements
For the Fiscal Year Ending
12/31/2020

Income Statement Period Ending	FYE 12/31/2019	% of Sales	FYE 12/31/2020	% of Sales	Notes/Comments ->
Sales Revenue:					
Professional Fees Billed	$7,750,000	88.89%	$3,955,000	93.02%	Impact of pandemic/large projects deferred.
Direct Expense Reimbursement	$968,750	11.11%	$296,625	6.98%	
Total Sales Revenue	$8,718,750	100.00%	$4,251,625	100.00%	
Costs of Sales:					
Personnel Wages & Burden	$2,615,625	30.00%	$1,381,778	32.50%	Sacrificed margin to maintain staff.
Subcontractors & Consultants	$1,612,969	18.50%	$850,325	20.00%	
Third Party Fees Incurred	$632,109	7.25%	$393,275	9.25%	
Total Costs of Sales	$4,860,703	55.75%	$2,625,378	61.75%	
Gross Profit & Gross Margin	$3,858,047	44.25%	$1,626,247	38.25%	Decrease anticipated.
Selling, Operating, & Administrative Expenses:					
Payroll, Wages, & Burden	$1,040,400	11.93%	$586,763	13.80%	Owners took 50% reduction in comp.
Advertising, Marketing, & Promotional	$395,400	4.54%	$126,450	2.97%	Low hanging fruit to cut/but need to increase.
Corporate Overhead & Professional Fees	$647,722	7.43%	$432,670	10.18%	Successfully subleased 30% of space.

(Continued)

EXHIBIT 6.1 (Continued)

Unaudited - Prepared by Company Management

Local Sample Service Co, Inc.
Unaudited Financial Statements
For the Fiscal Year Ending
12/31/2020

Income Statement Period Ending	FYE 12/31/2019	% of Sales	FYE 12/31/2020	% of Sales	Notes/Comments ->
Other Company Operating Expenses	$170,600	1.96%	$129,500	3.05%	Owners "travel" bucket/can be reduced.
Total Selling, Operating, & Admin. Expenses	$2,254,122	25.85%	$1,275,382	30.00%	
Operating Profit	$1,603,925	18.40%	$350,864	8.25%	
Other Expenses:					
Depreciation Expense	$39,156	0.45%	$39,156	0.92%	
Interest Expense	$9,790	0.11%	$10,877	0.26%	
Income Tax Expense	$800	0.01%	$800	0.02%	
Total Other Expenses	$49,746	0.57%	$50,834	1.20%	
Net Income (Loss)	$1,554,179	17.83%	$300,030	7.06%	
Additional Analysis & KPIs:					
Current Ratio	4.15		3.64		Well above minimum level of 2.5x.
Owners' Distributions (Exhibit 4.1 balance sheet)	$777,089		$777,089		Large distributions related to prior year profits.
Current Year Distributions % of Net Income	50.00%		259.00%		
Number of Professional Associates	16		10		Cut excess/inefficient staff. Maintained core.
Average Revenue Earned per Prof. Associate	$544,922		$425,163		Need minimum prod of $500k per. Should return.
Average Wages & Bonus per Prof. Associate	$125,751		$106,291		Down year due to general economic downturn.

Confidential - Property of Local Sample Service Co, Inc.

> ➤ We opted not to include the actual variance analysis as presented in Exhibit 4.3 but rather elected to include a notes or comments section as an example (which we previously alluded to in Chapter 4) to assist with understanding the financial results. The simple notes and comments now offer better insight into the company's financial performance and that even though 2020 was a difficult operating year, the company was able to pivot and implement business decisions to proactively adjust and still generate a small profit (with management being fully aware of the new economic reality).

We cannot emphasize enough that preparing and distributing reliable financial information is highly dependent on the target audience. In our example, the target audience is the ownership group of the company along with senior management. The ownership group needs to understand the company's financial results in an efficient and effective manner, without providing excessive amounts of detail or "noise." In one page or a simple snapshot, the owners need to clearly understand the company's financial performance or "story" with confidence so that executive-level business decisions can be made.

In our example, the owners may implement a financial performance objective that average earned revenue per professional associate must reach $500,000 in 2021, or further headcount reductions will be made (as this represents one of the company's critical KPIs).

For all businesses, it is imperative to remember who your audience is or will be when preparing financial information. Clearly understanding the business management chain of command is essential as senior- or executive-level parties will demand one type of financial information (i.e., macro-level and critical KPIs that really drive the financial results) versus mid-level or even lower managers who require more granular financial information to assess and manage a specific function.

BETTER LATE THAN NEVER, OKAY FOR EXTERNAL PARTIES

Timely financial information reporting has an entirely new meaning and value in today's rapid-fire economic environment. The ability to accumulate and analyze data, prepare financial information reports, and implement business decisions is more important today than ever before. Honestly, the topic of timely financial information reporting should not even be a discussion – if ever there was a no-brainer, this is it – but we would be remiss if we did not provide a bit more depth on the subject of timely financial information reporting as it relates to our two main audiences – external and internal parties.

Externally, reporting timelines are governed by regulatory or compliance requirements or by specific demands placed on a company by capital sources, investors, strategic partners, and similar parties. At a macro level, here are some of the more significant financial reporting timelines:

> *Taxation:* Filing dates for federal income tax returns are set by the IRS and vary by type of legal entity. For example, Subchapter S corporation returns are due on the 15th day of the third month following the fiscal year reporting period (e.g., March 15, 2021), whereas regular C corporation income tax returns are due 30 days later. However, companies may request an extension, which may provide as much as six more months of added time to file the income tax returns. Further, states generally adhere to the federal guidelines for filing business income tax returns but may implement their own policies. Confused yet? Well to be quite honest, income tax returns are just the tip of the iceberg as, between other federal, state, city, county, and local tax reporting (think payroll taxes, sales and use, property, excise, etc.), trying to keep track of all the reporting deadlines requirements can quickly become overwhelming. So, keep in mind the following three tips in understanding and managing tax reporting requirements.

- First, retain the services of a quality CPA firm or third-party tax specialty management company to assist with and administer tax reporting requirements. These groups have significant resources and experience to ensure that tax reporting requirements are responsibly managed.

- Second, the simpler or more specifically focused the tax, the quicker the filing requirement generally is. For example, sales taxes are generated on the sale of tangible goods, which are easy to calculate (what was the sales price and what is the tax rate?). Therefore, sales tax returns are often required to be filed every month, within 30 days of the previous month close of business.

- Third, and hugely important, understand the difference between a tax that is an expense of a business (e.g., property tax or income taxes) and taxes that are held in trust by the business and must be remitted to the taxing authority (e.g., sales tax and payroll tax withholdings). For taxes that are held in trust, the taxing authorities can get very nasty and aggressive when collecting and may pursue the officers, board members, and/or executives of a company at a personal level, if these taxes are not paid. This is known as "piercing the corporate veil," as not remitting taxes you have collected on behalf of a third party is an extremely sensitive issue.

➢ *Public Companies:* Financial information reporting timelines have been established by the SEC. A company's annual report (the 10K), including audited financial statements, is due within 60 or 90 days of the end of its fiscal year (depending on the size of the company). Similarly, a company's quarterly report (the 10Q), including unaudited financial statements, is due within 35 to 45 days of the previous quarter end (depending on size). The SEC has established other reporting timelines as well for miscellaneous business activity that must be communicated to the public in a timely fashion. Basically, all public companies secure the best CPA firms and legal counsel to support this effort.

➢ *Private Companies:* The banks, lenders, and investors of private companies will almost always demand that financial information be reported within set time frames. Unlike public companies (that have specific rules established by the SEC), the financial information reporting time frames for private companies are established in specific agreements executed between two parties. For example, a bank may require that a company provide internal financial statements or covenant compliance calculations within 120 days of the fiscal year-end, a borrowing base certificate within 30 days of the month end, or a business valuation within 180 days of a specific date (e.g., the original loan date). The list of potential financial information reporting and associated timelines is endless, but the general rule of thumb is that the higher the perceived risk of investment loss from a third party, the quicker and more complete the financial reporting.

You may ask why we went to this effort to overview various external reporting requirements, as it should be evident that timeliness for external reporting requirements is really not all that timely. And that is the point, as external reporting timelines are based more on compliance than business management and planning needs. External parties seem to be forever behind the curve as by the time these groups receive the financial information, 30 to 180 days after the fact, the industries in which they operate or even the world (e.g., the COVID-19 outbreak in 2020) may have changed with all eyes now focused on the future rather than the past.

BETTER LATE THAN NEVER DOES NOT FLY INTERNALLY!

Speed is everything in today's fast-paced business world, but let us take a moment to remember the all-important acronym GIGO (which, if you have forgotten, stands for garbage in – garbage out). Simply put, if your accounting system has failed and cannot be relied on to produce accurate information, then the timeliness of your financial information reporting will be all for naught. We wanted to emphasize this point as while timely financial information reporting is critical, it should not be undertaken at the expense of producing accurate, reliable, and complete financial information. All businesses must find that right balance between speed, accuracy, and reliability when producing internal financial information and reports.

With this said, let us turn our attention to better understanding how companies produce timely financial information in somewhat of a chronological order (fastest to slowest).

➢ Hourly (or even more frequent): You would be amazed at how many companies now produce internal financial information and reports on an hourly or even more frequent basis. For example, during the critical holiday selling season for retailers, sales data can be accumulated on demand, thanks to advancements in technology. The effectiveness of an advertising campaign can almost immediately be evaluated by companies selling products direct to consumers (DTC) as they can literally monitor, in real time, consumer reactions to different promotions (and make changes as needed). This type of financial information is generally reported via "flash reports" (refer to Chapter 11) and is centered on accumulating data that is more efficiently obtained and deciphered (e.g., total sales, total units sold, and average unit selling price). The idea is to not overwhelm the user with excessive amounts of data, calculations, and so on, but rather "flash" three to five pieces of key financial information that relays the message (loud and clear).

➢ Daily: Daily reporting is now the norm in several industries and once again, you can thank technology for making this happen. Here, certain data points or key operating metrics are accumulated for a day or similar period to take a snapshot of the operating performance. A perfect example of daily reporting resides in the restaurant industry, as companies can evaluate total sales by type, costs of sales, personnel expenses, and key efficiency ratios to monitor like-period performances or determine whether staffing levels are too high or too low. Unlike the flash reports noted above, daily reporting requires more data or source inputs to support a management evaluation of operating results so the reporting timelines, instead of an hour, are often reviewed one day in arrears (to provide a small window for a scrubbing by the accounting team).

➢ Weekly: Moving down the reporting timeline food chain we arrive at weekly financial reporting. Similar to daily reporting requiring more data inputs than hourly, weekly follows the same logic. A couple of prime examples of weekly reporting are centered in a production manager analyzing the prior week's manufacturing targets or quotas (based on volume, product type, and quality assurance) or a weekly cash flow analysis that reports beginning cash, total inflows, total outflows, and ending cash. Data or source inputs are more voluminous, volatile, and tend to be somewhat more complex, so a company may elect for weekly reporting to smooth out certain variances or ensure that a set of transactions scheduled for once a week are captured (e.g., a company may only pay its vendors once a week, on each Friday). By the way, the reason we referenced weekly cash flow reporting is that for companies that may be operating under elevated business stress levels, with limited financial capital and tight cash balances, weekly monitoring of available cash is essential. Companies often utilize a 13- or 26-week rolling cash flow report to monitor cash inflows and outflows, and to determine exactly when cash stress will be at its peak. This helps the company's management team look forward and plan accordingly, including tapping vendors that can be "leaned on" to defer payments (helping free up cash for a short window) or identifying customers who might be able to accelerate payments.

➢ Monthly: The big three financial statements offer a perfect example of monthly financial information reporting. When we discuss financial statement reporting throughout this book, annual or quarterly financial statement reporting is generally being referenced but it should be noted that almost all companies produce financial statements monthly (given the importance of the financial results to the owners, management team, capital sources, etc.). Given the added complexity of the financial statements along with the large number of data or source inputs, monthly financial statements are the norm (as producing more frequently is difficult). Also, internally prepared financial statements are usually produced in a much quicker time frame than financial statements prepared for external distribution. This provides management with plenty of time to review, analyze, scrub, adjust (if needed), prepare, and present to external parties.

➤ Quarterly and Annual: Financial statements represent an example of quarterly and annual financial information reporting in addition to a wide range of other requirements, including preparing quarterly or annual operating budgets and financial forecasts (refer to Chapter 10) or specialized financial analyses that require large amounts of data accumulated over a long time period (such as auto companies evaluating the amount of a warranty reserve for a new product line or a distribution company analyzing slow-moving inventory). If you had not noticed moving down our financial reporting timeline, the less frequent the reporting requirement usually is associated with a higher likelihood that the financial information will be distributed to external parties. It is both pointless and foolish to distribute frequently prepared financial information and reports (i.e., hourly, daily, and weekly) to external parties that may confuse the external party, is confidential in nature, and that has not been properly vetted by management.

Additional examples of the types of business financial information reporting could be provided, as the potential list of reports is endless. The primary concept to remember is that it is up to the company's management team to determine what financial information is needed, for whom, and when it is needed to ensure that critical information is provided to executives and managers on which to base sound business decisions.

We should also note that effective business reporting is just as important in evaluating operational or qualitative matters as with financial results. Employee turnover (critical to the hospitality industry), customer service requests and complaints, and average customer response times offer just a few examples. It is beyond the scope of this book to dig deeper into these types of business reporting requirements, but we did want to mention them as, in some capacity, they all will have an impact on a company's financial results.

RELIABILITY, TIMELINESS, AND THE FINANCIAL STORY

A subject matter that is near and dear to our hearts warrants a brief discussion as we close out this chapter; that is, how does reliability and timeliness translate into assisting the executive management team with properly relaying and communicating the business and economic financial story and opportunity to a target audience?

As an example, a company that is growing rapidly and wants to specifically call attention to a segment of the business that has perceived high value by external parties will want to structure or format its external financial reports and statements to help "tell (or sell) the story." Management may specifically tailor or structure the financial information to support the business story in the most attractive manner possible and then deliver the information at the opportune time. For the ideal external audience, the reliability and timeliness of the financial information is strategically prepared and distributed to achieve an optimum outcome. If you need further insight on this concept just think about the large number of IPOs that took place in late 2020, riding on the tailwinds of very robust public markets and the impact on business models resulting from COVID-19. The story fit perfectly as did the timing of the IPO.

Internally, the company should be just as motivated to ensure that reliable and timely financial information is prepared for management review and analysis. But here, the audience is different so the financial story (at a micro level) will need to be tailored as necessary, keeping in mind just how confidential the financial information can be and the need to tightly control sensitive data.

In either case, the goal remains the same, as the focus is to assist your audience with understanding financial information and operating results in an efficient, effective, and controlled manner and that the financial information story aligns with the macro-level business opportunity story.

You will better understand just how important it is to effectively communicate a business opportunity, in a reliable and timely fashion, when we enter discussions on raising capital (Chapter 13) and valuing a business (Chapter 15).

CHAPTER 7

Business Cycles and Financial Connections

OUR COMPANION BOOK – *HOW TO READ A FINANCIAL REPORT*

The concept of accounting cycles and connections between the financial statements is covered at length in a companion book we authored, titled *How to Read a Financial Report*. This book, now in its ninth edition with hundreds of thousands of copies sold, dedicates eight chapters in Part Two to providing detailed explanations of how the financial information presented in an income statement is linked or connected to the balance sheet, how financial information presented in the balance sheet is linked or connected to the statement of cash flows, and so on. For those of you who would like to dig deeper into understanding accounting connections at a more granular level, we would encourage you to read *How to Read a Financial Report* with a specific focus on Chapters 5 through 12.

In this chapter, we will also be covering the topic of financial information connections but will approach the subject from a different perspective. First, *How to Read a Financial Report* explains financial information connections from more of a technical accounting perspective or based on when an actual financial transaction has taken place (the sale of products to a customer). We will expand on this topic by looking at all financial transactions associated with business cycles from soup to nuts (i.e., the entire sales cycle). Second, we will expand our discussion on financial information connections by taking it up a notch to help you understand the flow of financial information transactions from start to finish for a specific cycle. Our goal is to expand and enhance your knowledge of financial information from the basics (e.g., a sale of a product to a customer on credit creates revenue for the company as well as a trade receivable) to being slightly more sophisticated to understanding a business cycle from birth to death.

We will limit our discussion to covering four primary financial business cycles: the sales cycle, the purchasing cycle, the operating expense cycle, and the investment and financing cycle (which are closely related). Other financial business cycles exist but for most companies, the four cycles overviewed in this chapter cover the bulk of financial transactions and will help you understand how financial information moves inside a company and where it originates. We should also note that the exhibits presented in this chapter are going to be more detailed, as they relate to documenting the flow of transactions for an entire business cycle. Whereas in *How to Read a Financial Report* a single financial connection was presented, in this chapter four to five financial connections (referred to as financial flows) are presented to account for a business cycle rather than a single accounting transaction. So be patient with our presentation and review the material as needed to enhance your knowledge of these critical business cycles.

THE SALES CYCLE

The entire purpose of a business is to develop a plan that offers a product or service to the market that customers value and that will allow the business to earn a profit. This process starts at the top of the income statement where sales revenue is reported. But the selling process or cycle is far more complex than the top line of the income statement would lead you to believe, as before any company makes a sale, it must create a business plan, raise capital to execute the business plan, invest in infrastructure to implement the business plan, develop products or services the market will place a value on, market or promote these products or services to potential customers, then actually complete or close a sale with the customer (triggering sales revenue in the income statement), and finally properly support and service the customer (ensuring they become "sticky" or repeat customers). The concept of customer retention is extremely important for all companies, as we are not aware of any successful business that has not been able to sell products or services, over and over, to the same customer. Just think about Apple, Inc. for a moment and their ability to sell new versions of the iPhone to existing customers year after year. Without having dedicated and loyal customers (i.e., sticky), Apple would have been out of business decades ago.

This is what we mean by the sales cycle, as companies will incur numerous operating expenses both before a sale is made (e.g., spending money on advertising) and after it is completed (e.g., investing in a service center to respond to customer questions, technical support needs, etc.). Exhibit 7.1 helps visualize the entire sales cycle from the perspective of accounting connections between the income statement and the balance sheet. We have compressed the financial statements further to keep the presentation on one page for ease of review highlighting four primary information flows.

1. The first financial information flow captures the various operating expenses incurred to support the direct selling, marketing, and promotional efforts prior to a sale being made or with customer service costs after the sale. These expenses would generally first be captured as a trade payable (e.g., advertising spends with a social media company to be paid in 30 days) or an accrued liability (e.g., staff wages payable) until a cash payment is made per the terms established by the supplier.

2. The second financial information flow captures a simple sale between the company and a customer for the delivery of products. In this case, the company provides 30-day payment terms to the customer so the sale would be captured as a trade account receivable until the customer pays.

3. The third financial information flow is a bit different as it captures an advance billing to a customer for a software service to be provided over the next 12 months (e.g., a SaaS sale). The customer is billed for the software service in advance, which is recorded as a trade account receivable, but not GAAP sales revenue, as the company must defer recognizing the earned revenue over a 12-month period. Rather, the billing is captured as an other current liability or deferred revenue on the balance sheet. The customer would eventually remit payment just like in flow 2.

4. The fourth financial information flow is presented to reflect the fact that over a period of 12 months, the other current liability or deferred revenue would be reduced and sales revenue increased as the company fulfills its obligation for the advance billing and earns a prorated portion of the software service sale. What is interesting about this transaction is that (unlike the other three) cash will not be impacted, as the customer should have paid the advance billing long ago.

EXHIBIT 7.1   Sales Cycle Financial Transaction Flows

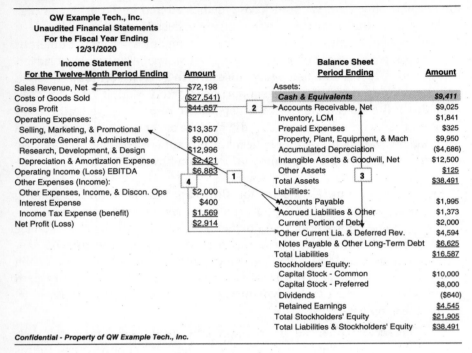

QW Example Tech., Inc. Unaudited Financial Statements For the Fiscal Year Ending 12/31/2020				
Income Statement For the Twelve-Month Period Ending	**Amount**		**Balance Sheet** Period Ending	**Amount**
Sales Revenue, Net	$72,198		Assets:	
Costs of Goods Sold	($27,541)		*Cash & Equivalents*	*$9,411*
Gross Profit	$44,657	2	Accounts Receivable, Net	$9,025
Operating Expenses:			Inventory, LCM	$1,841
Selling, Marketing, & Promotional	$13,357		Prepaid Expenses	$325
Corporate General & Administrative	$9,000		Property, Plant, Equipment, & Mach	$9,950
Research, Development, & Design	$12,996		Accumulated Depreciation	($4,686)
Depreciation & Amortization Expense	$2,421		Intangible Assets & Goodwill, Net	$12,500
Operating Income (Loss) EBITDA	$6,883	1	Other Assets	$125
Other Expenses (Income):		4	Total Assets	3	$38,491
Other Expenses, Income, & Discon. Ops	$2,000		Liabilities:	
Interest Expense	$400		Accounts Payable	$1,995
Income Tax Expense (benefit)	$1,569		Accrued Liabilities & Other	$1,373
Net Profit (Loss)	$2,914		Current Portion of Debt	$2,000
			Other Current Lia. & Deferred Rev.	$4,594
			Notes Payable & Other Long-Term Debt	$6,625
			Total Liabilities	$16,587
			Stockholders' Equity:	
			Capital Stock - Common	$10,000
			Capital Stock - Preferred	$8,000
			Dividends	($640)
			Retained Earnings	$4,545
			Total Stockholders' Equity	$21,905
			Total Liabilities & Stockholders' Equity	$38,491

We have bolded the cash account for the simple purpose of emphasizing that for financial information flows 1, 2, and 3, the result of the transactions will always clear through cash (as vendors are paid and customers remit payments). Financial flow 4 helps explain how sales revenue is earned from a different type of customer billing that is based on establishing an accounting policy to properly recognize earned sales revenue over an appropriate period.

Exhibit 7.1 was presented to help you understand that recording sales revenue in the income statement is not as simple as billing a customer for the delivery of a product or service (and waiting to get paid). We specifically noted in Chapter 5 that revenue recognition represents a hot topic when issuing GAAP financial statements and is something all companies must clearly understand and proactively manage to ensure that external and internal parties are not misled. This goes back to why we emphasized understanding the entire sales cycle (and not just connections) from an accounting perspective, as it is not always black-and-white (gray, as in a gray area, would be our favorite choice of color here).

It should also be noted that for most companies, the selling cycle (from conceptualizing a product or service for sale through to turning customers into repeat buyers) is almost always longer than anticipated and requires more management attention and financial capital to support. So plan accordingly and make sure you have plenty of capital, as there is nothing worse than almost reaching the promised land and then having the door slammed shut.

THE PURCHASING CYCLE

Our focus on the purchasing cycle will be geared toward costs of goods sold (for product-related companies) or costs of sales (for service-based companies). And like the sales cycle, the purchasing cycle is much more complex than simply buying or manufacturing products and selling them to the customer. You cannot understand the purchasing cycle without including a discussion on developing and managing the supply chain. Both product and service-driven companies must manage supply chains that can be extraordinarily complex and far-reaching in terms of coordinating a vast pool of suppliers, vendors, staff, and other third parties to ensure that the right product or service is available for sale to the right parties at the right time. Speak to anyone who is involved with the supply chain and you will quickly understand just how much effort and resources it takes, for even a small company selling 30 different products, to manage effectively. Compounding management of the supply chain is that in today's global economy, companies are now, more than ever, having to coordinate vendors, suppliers, and employees that span the globe. This is why the purchasing cycle and supply chain incur significant amounts of operating expenses, both prior to receiving the product and long after the product has been sold.

Exhibit 7.2 presents the purchasing cycle and the accounting connections in a more complete fashion. We have compressed the financial statements further to keep the presentation on one page for ease of review highlighting four primary information flows.

1. The first financial information flow captures the various operating expenses incurred to support any product research and development costs, management team expenses related to managing the supply chain, and so on, prior to a product or service being made available

EXHIBIT 7.2   Purchasing Cycle Financial Transaction Flows

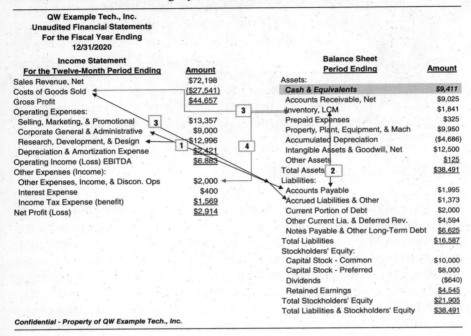

QW Example Tech., Inc.
Unaudited Financial Statements
For the Fiscal Year Ending
12/31/2020

Income Statement For the Twelve-Month Period Ending	Amount
Sales Revenue, Net	$72,198
Costs of Goods Sold	($27,541)
Gross Profit	$44,657
Operating Expenses:	
Selling, Marketing, & Promotional	$13,357
Corporate General & Administrative	$9,000
Research, Development, & Design	$12,996
Depreciation & Amortization Expense	$2,421
Operating Income (Loss) EBITDA	$6,883
Other Expenses (Income):	
Other Expenses, Income, & Discon. Ops	$2,000
Interest Expense	$400
Income Tax Expense (benefit)	$1,569
Net Profit (Loss)	$2,914

Balance Sheet Period Ending	Amount
Assets:	
Cash & Equivalents	$9,411
Accounts Receivable, Net	$9,025
Inventory, LCM	$1,841
Prepaid Expenses	$325
Property, Plant, Equipment, & Mach	$9,950
Accumulated Depreciation	($4,686)
Intangible Assets & Goodwill, Net	$12,500
Other Assets	$125
Total Assets	$38,491
Liabilities:	
Accounts Payable	$1,995
Accrued Liabilities & Other	$1,373
Current Portion of Debt	$2,000
Other Current Lia. & Deferred Rev.	$4,594
Notes Payable & Other Long-Term Debt	$6,625
Total Liabilities	$16,587
Stockholders' Equity:	
Capital Stock - Common	$10,000
Capital Stock - Preferred	$8,000
Dividends	($640)
Retained Earnings	$4,545
Total Stockholders' Equity	$21,905
Total Liabilities & Stockholders' Equity	$38,491

Confidential - Property of QW Example Tech., Inc.

for sale or subsequent vendor management expenses. These expenses would generally first be captured as a trade payable (e.g., trial product sample order with a vendor that is to be paid in 30 days) or an accrued liability (e.g., staff wages payable) until a cash payment is made per the terms established by the supplier.

2. The second financial information flow is between balance sheet accounts only, as before a product can be sold it must be purchased, which is often done on supplier-provided terms. For example, if a company purchases 10,000 units of a product, which are received and made available for sale, the inventory account would increase along with a trade account payable to the supplier (which may provide payment terms of 30 or 60 days). There is no impact on the income statement yet as until a product is sold, it would not be recorded as a cost of goods sold.

3. Two financial information flows are captured in our third connection. These are the actual cost of a product being sold (which would reduce

the value in inventory and increase the costs of goods sold) as well as any other direct costs of sales that might be incurred, such as rent on a building used to produce the products, or staff wages and burden for employees who are involved with producing the products. This is why we referenced two connections; while selling a product reduces inventory, costs of sales may also increase trade accounts payable or accrued liabilities.

4. Finally, we could not resist including a fourth connection that specifically relates to our sample company. We cover this topic in more depth in Chapter 14, but what our sample company elected to do was to write off certain inventory that was deemed to be worthless. Rather than record this inventory write-off as costs of goods sold, the company elected to reflect the write-off as a one-time nonrecurring expense and record it as other expenses (so that its gross profit and gross margin were not adversely affected). This write-off represents a noncash expense as somewhere in the past the company did have to use cash to purchase the inventory (flow 2 in Exhibit 7.2), when the election to write off the inventory represented an accounting entry (to reduce inventory and increase other expenses).

Exhibit 7.2 was presented to help you understand that purchasing or making products for sale (or delivering services to the customer) is not as simple as placing an order for the delivery of the product or service (and waiting for a customer to purchase it). The entire purchasing and supply chain cycle is complex, expensive to manage, and requires a great deal of coordination between multiple parties. Keeping this in mind, we can offer two pieces of advice in relation to understanding the purchasing cycle and supply chain better.

First, disruptions to the supply chain are the rule rather than the exception. It is inevitable that somewhere along the line, an adverse event will occur that requires responsive management actions. Second, if there has ever been an area in a business that relies on clear and concise communication skills, this is it. Technology is not a cure-all or replacement for a function that lives and dies on being able to effectively communicate.

THE OPERATING EXPENSE CYCLE

The operating expense cycle has been touched on with our discussions on the sales and purchasing cycles, so we are not going to expend a significant amount of additional time on this cycle. If you refer to Exhibits 7.1 and 7.2, the first financial information flow captures the essence of operating expenses as it relates to the impact on the current liabilities section of the balance sheet (including trade accounts payable and accrued liabilities). Most, but not all, operating expenses tend to flow through a company's financial statements in this fashion, where the expense is incurred during a period but paid later.

Operating expenses capture a wide range of business expenses that companies incur to support ongoing operations and include the following items (in no specific order):

> ➤ Rental of office buildings, copiers, trucks and autos, telephone system equipment, computers, and other assets.
> ➤ Utility costs of electricity, water, sewage, and so on.
> ➤ Wages, salaries, commissions, bonuses, and other compensation paid to managers, office staff, salespersons, warehouse workers, security guards, and other employees. (Compensation of production employees and associated benefits such as payroll taxes are included in the costs of goods manufactured and become part of inventory cost.)
> ➤ Payroll taxes and fringe benefit costs of labor, such as health and medical plan contributions by the employer and the cost of employee retirement plans (associated with non-productive staff).
> ➤ Professional fees for legal, accounting, human resources, and so on.
> ➤ Office and data processing supplies, telecommunication expenses, Internet, and website costs.
> ➤ Dues and subscriptions such as software platform expenses.
> ➤ Liability, fire, accident, and other insurance costs.
> ➤ Marketing, advertising, and sales promotion costs, which are major expenditures by many businesses.
> ➤ Travel, meals, lodging, and entertainment costs.

This list is not all-inclusive. We are sure you could think of many more expenses of operating a business. Even relatively small businesses keep 100 or more separate accounts for specific operating expenses. Larger business corporations keep thousands of specific expense accounts. In their external financial reports, however, most publicly owned corporations report only one, two, or three operating expense categories.

From an accounting perspective, some operating expenses are recorded when they are paid, not before or after. An example of this relates to companies that remit payments daily to social media advertising platforms such as Facebook. Each day the company expends $X of advertising, which is paid via a direct payment from their bank account to Facebook, usually via an electronic remittance (e.g., ACH). It would be convenient if every dollar of operating expenses were a dollar actually paid out in the same period. But, as this and later chapters demonstrate, running a business is not so simple. The point is that for many operating expenses a business cannot wait to record the expense until it pays the expense. As soon as a liability is incurred, the amount of expense should be recorded. The term *incurred* means that the business has a definite responsibility to pay a third party that has a legal claim against the business.

A liability is incurred when a company takes on an obligation to make future payment and has received the economic benefit of the cost in operating the business. Recording the liability for an unpaid expense is one fundamental aspect of *accrual-basis accounting*. Expenses are *accrued* (i.e., recorded before they are paid) so that the amount of each expense is deducted from sales revenue to measure profit correctly for the period.

Two final thoughts related to the operating expense cycle: First, certain operating expenses may be prepaid for an operating period. For example, general liability insurance coverage is often paid upfront for the entire year the policy covers. Per GAAP, this expense should be recorded as a prepaid asset (under the classification of prepaid expenses in the current asset section of the balance sheet) and amortized or expensed over the appropriate 12-month period. This is the opposite of most operating expenses as it is paid in advance (before it was incurred) as opposed to being incurred and then paid later.

Second, strong accounting policies, procedures, and internal controls must be established by a company to ensure that not only are all expenses accounted for in the correct period (whether paid or not) but just as importantly, the expenses are properly recorded to the correct account in the accounting system. There is nothing worse than having to sort through financial information that is polluted with incorrect coding of expenses.

THE INVESTMENT AND FINANCING CYCLES

Our final stop with business cycles lands us with the investment and financing cycles. We have combined our discussion on these two subjects given their close association (e.g., to make a large investment in assets the company must be able to finance the investment) and importance. And yes, like our discussions on the sales and purchasing cycles, it will quickly become apparent that the investment and financing cycle is both complex and time-consuming, dependent on a strong business foundation and plan to support or justify the economic feasibility of the investment, and that the required financial capital is appropriate to support the investment.

The start of the investment and financing cycle starts with a plan. It does not matter if the plan has been prepared to launch a new business or is associated with a large company looking to invest in a new manufacturing facility. A plan must be developed that is well supported at multiple levels, including market feasibility, operational effectiveness, environmental and legal compliance, and economic justification, just to highlight some major components. Developing a plan takes a significant amount of time, resources, and management attention, which again brings us to the start of the process in that operating expenses will be incurred well before any investment decision is made and financial capital pursued. Then, only if it is deemed economically justifiable to proceed will investment and financing decisions be made.

Exhibit 7.3 summarizes the primary financial flows related to the investment and financing cycle. We have compressed the financial statements further to keep the presentation on one page for ease of review, highlighting four primary financial information flows.

1. The first financial information flow captures the various operating expenses incurred to develop the investment plan, including management team expenses, professional fees incurred to help build the plan, and so on. These expenses would generally first be captured as a trade payable (e.g., a marketing consulting company that completed a feasibility study providing 90-day payment terms) or an accrued liability (e.g., staff wages payable) until a cash payment is made per the terms established by the supplier.

2. Second, the financial information flow highlights the fact that our sample company raised financial capital (and received cash) in the form of debt and equity to support the proposed investment. Although possible, it is highly unlikely that an investment in an asset is going to

EXHIBIT 7.3 The Investment and Financing Financial Transaction Flows

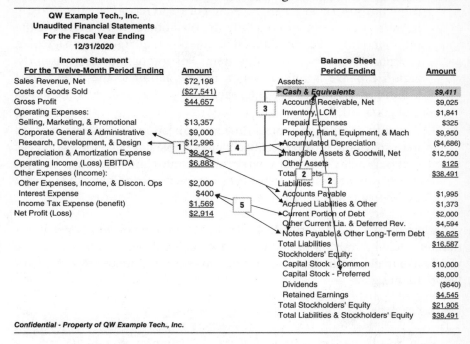

QW Example Tech., Inc.
Unaudited Financial Statements
For the Fiscal Year Ending
12/31/2020

Income Statement For the Twelve-Month Period Ending	Amount
Sales Revenue, Net	$72,198
Costs of Goods Sold	($27,541)
Gross Profit	$44,657
Operating Expenses:	
Selling, Marketing, & Promotional	$13,357
Corporate General & Administrative	$9,000
Research, Development, & Design	$12,996
Depreciation & Amortization Expense	$8,421
Operating Income (Loss) EBITDA	$6,883
Other Expenses (Income):	
Other Expenses, Income, & Discon. Ops	$2,000
Interest Expense	$400
Income Tax Expense (benefit)	$1,569
Net Profit (Loss)	$2,914

Balance Sheet Period Ending	Amount
Assets:	
Cash & Equivalents	$9,411
Accounts Receivable, Net	$9,025
Inventory, LCM	$1,841
Prepaid Expenses	$325
Property, Plant, Equipment, & Mach	$9,950
Accumulated Depreciation	($4,686)
Intangible Assets & Goodwill, Net	$12,500
Other Assets	$125
Total Assets	$38,491
Liabilities:	
Accounts Payable	$1,995
Accrued Liabilities & Other	$1,373
Current Portion of Debt	$2,000
Other Current Lia. & Deferred Rev.	$4,594
Notes Payable & Other Long-Term Debt	$6,625
Total Liabilities	$16,587
Stockholders' Equity:	
Capital Stock - Common	$10,000
Capital Stock - Preferred	$8,000
Dividends	($640)
Retained Earnings	$4,545
Total Stockholders' Equity	$21,905
Total Liabilities & Stockholders' Equity	$38,491

Confidential - Property of QW Example Tech., Inc.

be made without having the proper financial capital secured. At this point, the only impact is in the balance sheet, as cash, notes payable, and preferred equity balances all increased.

3. Third, our flow captures that with cash in hand, the company has made a significant investment in an intangible asset to support their aggressive business plan and drive to increase software sales. Again, only a balance sheet impact is present, as the cash that was raised was used to make a significant purchase of $12.5 million in intangible assets.

4. Fourth, we finally see a financial information flow that connects the balance sheet with the income statement in the form of depreciation and amortization expense. When companies invest in either tangible (e.g., machinery or equipment) or intangible (e.g., patents or trade secrets) assets, it is assumed that over a period of time these assets will be consumed and lose value. For tangible assets, businesses must record depreciation expense on a periodic basis to recognize the reduction in value (as the asset is consumed). For intangible

assets, businesses generally record amortization expense (for the same purpose) over an appropriate period to recognize the decrease in value. In our sample company, depreciation expense increases the total amount of accumulated depreciation (since inception), which is reported on a separate line item. For intangible assets, amortization expense is reflected as a net reduction to the asset value. This is why you see the reference to "Net" after intangible assets and goodwill.

5. Our fifth and final financial flow or connection ties interest expense to the current and long-term debt our sample has outstanding. It goes without saying that loans carry interest rates and associated interest expense to the connection between company debt or loans and interest expense should be logical.

Chapters 13 and 17 provide a significant amount of additional information related to raising capital from both debt and equity sources, but we would like to close our discussion on the investing and financing cycle with two final thoughts.

 First, the financing cycle is usually an extremely intensive process that is time-consuming, exhausting, frustrating, and stressful. Remember that it is one thing to come up with a plan and get in front of the right financing source, hoping that they display some level of interest; it is something completely different to convince the financing source to "write the check" and commit real capital to the investment opportunity.

Second, be prepared for rejection, which you should not take personally. Securing financing, whether for a new start-up company or for an internal business expansion, is one of the most challenging aspects of operating a business and one of the primary reasons there are so few real entrepreneurs in relation to the number of people working in the marketplace. If it were easy, everyone would be doing it – and trust us when we say, securing financing is anything but easy.

PART TWO

HOW TO ANALYZE FINANCIAL INFORMATION AND ITS MEANING

CHAPTER 8

Basic Financial Ratio Analysis and Terminology

PURPOSE AND STANDARD TERMINOLOGY

Whether from an internal or external perspective, financial ratio analysis represents an invaluable tool to help assess how a company is performing financially. External parties rely heavily on completing detailed financial ratio analyses to evaluate the economic performance of a company but often deal with two limiting factors. First, external parties generally can only complete their analyses on an annual or quarterly basis (when financial reports are issued). Second, and more importantly, external parties do not have access to the same amount of confidential or detailed financial information as internal management (which enables internal management to complete a more thorough and informative analysis). Internal management can dig deeper and complete financial ratio analyses more frequently, but make no mistake – these are tools that are essential for both internal and external parties!

Before we provide a listing of what are considered the standard or basic financial ratio analyses, it will be helpful to walk through a list of commonly used financial and accounting terminology (to ensure that you are well versed with financial lingo):

➤ Top Line: A company's net sales revenue generated over a period of time (e.g., for a 12-month period).

➤ COGS or COS: Pronounced like it is spelled; stands for costs of goods sold (for a product-based business) and costs of sales (for a service-based business). COGS or COS tend to vary directly (or in a linear fashion) with the top-line sales revenue.

➤ Gross Profit and Margin: Sometimes used interchangeably, gross profit equals your top line less your COGS or COS. The gross margin (a percentage calculation) is determined by dividing your gross profit by the top line.

➤ Op Ex: Is a rather broad term that is short for operating expenses, which may include selling, general, administrative, corporate overhead, and other related expenses. Unlike COGS or COS, Op Ex tends to be fixed in nature and will not vary directly with the top-line sales revenue.

➤ SG&A: Selling, general, and administrative expenses. Companies may distinguish between Op Ex and SG&A to assist parties with understanding the expense structure of its operations in more detail.

➤ Bottom Line: A company's net profit or loss after all expenses have been deducted from net sales revenue. Being in the "black" indicates that a net profit is present and being in the "red" indicates that a net loss was generated.

➤ Breakeven: The operating level where a company generates zero in profit or loss as it "broke even." Or, conversely, it is the amount of sales revenue that needs to be generated to cover all COGS/COS and Op Ex.

➤ Contribution Margin: You may hear companies reference the term *contribution margin*. What this generally refers to is the profit generated by a specific operating unit or division of a company (but not for the company as a whole). Most larger companies have multiple operating units or divisions, so the profit (or loss) of each operating unit or division is calculated to determine how much that specific unit or division "contributed" to the overall performance of the entire company.

➤ Cap Ex: While Op Ex is associated with the income statement, Cap Ex stands for capital expenditures and is a calculation of how much a company invested in tangible or intangible assets during a given period (for equipment, machinery, new buildings, investments in intangible assets, etc.).

➤ YTD, QTD, MTD: These are simple and stand for year to date, quarter to date, or month to date. For example, a flash report may present QTD sales for the period of 10/1/20 through 11/15/20 (so management can evaluate sales levels through the middle of a quarter).

> ➤ FYE and QE: These two items stand for fiscal year-end and quarter-end. Most companies utilize a fiscal year-end that is consistent with a calendar year-end of 12/31/xx (which would make their quarter-ends 3/31/xx, 6/30/xx, 9/30/xx, and 12/31/xx). Please note that several companies utilize FYEs that are different than a calendar year-end to match their business cycle with that of a specific industry. For example, companies that cater to the education industry may use an FYE of 6/30/xx to coincide with the typical operating year for schools or colleges (which tend to run from 7/1/xx through 6/30/xx).

A BIT MORE DEPTH ON OUR CASE STUDY BUSINESS

Our fictitious case study company (i.e., QW Example Tech., Inc.) referenced throughout this book is a technology-based business that elected to pivot from selling tangible computers and high-tech equipment (along with certain software) to selling software platforms marketed and distributed through a subscription-based model (e.g., customers pay for an annual subscription that the company bills in advance). Management elected to make this change in 2019 based on changing market conditions and fully implemented the revised business plan in 2020 (by making a significant acquisition of technology in the amount of $12.5 million).

Our fictitious company is privately owned and has two primary types of equity, common and preferred stock. Neither its common nor preferred stock ownership shares are traded in public markets. The business has approximately 50 shareholders; some are company insiders (e.g., executive management including the CEO, the president, and several vice presidents) and others are independent investors (such as a venture capitalist or private equity group). A business this size could go into the public marketplace for equity capital through an initial public offering (IPO) of capital stock shares and become publicly owned. However, the company has decided to remain private.

This chapter does not pretend to cover the field of *securities analysis* (i.e., the analysis of stocks and debt instruments issued by corporations), but this is a topic touched on in Chapters 13 and 17. The broad field of securities analysis includes the analysis of competitive advantages and disadvantages of a business, domestic and international economic developments, business combination possibilities, general economic conditions, and much more. The key ratios explained in this chapter are basic building blocks in securities analysis.

Also, this chapter does not discuss *trend analysis*, which involves comparing a company's latest financial statements with its previous years' statements to identify important year-to-year changes. For example, investors and lenders are extremely interested in the sales growth or decline of a business, and the resulting impact on profit performance, cash flow, and financial condition. The concept of trend analysis is touched on in Chapter 3 and again in Chapter 10 (covering forecasts).

This chapter has a more modest objective – to explain basic ratios used in financial statement analysis and what those ratios indicate about a business. Only a handful of ratios are discussed in the chapter, but they are fundamentally important and represent the most widely used by industry professionals.

On opening a company's financial report, probably one of the first things most investors do is to give the financial statements the once-over. What do most financial report readers first look for? In our experience, they look first at the bottom line of the income statement, to see if the business made a profit or suffered a loss for the year. As one sports celebrity put it when explaining how he keeps tabs on his various business investments, he looks first to see if the bottom line has "parentheses around it." The business in our example does not; it made a profit. Its income statement reports that the business earned $2,914,000 (rounded; see Exhibit 3.1) net income, or bottom-line profit for the year. Is this profit performance good, mediocre, or poor? Ratios help answer this question.

After reading the income statement, most financial statement readers probably then take a quick look at the company's assets and compare them with the liabilities of the business. Are the assets adequate to the demands of the company's liabilities? Again, ratios help answer this question.

BENCHMARK FINANCIAL RATIOS – FINANCIAL STRENGTH AND SOLVENCY

Stock analysts, investment managers, individual investors, investment bankers, economists, company directors and executive management teams, and many others are interested in the fundamental financial aspects of a business. Ratios are a big help in analyzing the financial situation and performance of a business. To start our discussion on financial ratio analysis, you might be anticipating that we will begin with profit analysis. No, we start with something more important – solvency and liquidity.

Solvency and liquidity refer to the ability of a business to pay its liabilities when they come due. If a business is insolvent and cannot pay its liabilities on time, its very continuance is at stake. In many respects, solvency comes first and profit second (as the first rule in business is to never run out of cash to operate). The ability to earn a profit rests on the ability of the business to continue on course and avoid being shut down or interfered with by its lenders. In short, earning a profit demands that a business remain solvent. Maintaining solvency (its debt-paying ability) is essential for every business. If a business defaults on its debt obligations, it becomes vulnerable to legal proceedings that could stop the company in its tracks, or at least could interfere with its normal operations.

Bankers and other lenders, when deciding whether to make and renew loans to a business, direct their attention to certain key financial statement ratios to help them evaluate the solvency situation and prospects of the business. These ratios provide a useful financial profile of the business in assessing its creditworthiness and for judging the ability of the business to pay interest and to repay the principal of its loans on time and in full.

One additional concept that is important to understand is the difference between solvency and liquidity. In certain cases, you may evaluate a business that appears solvent (i.e., assets are greater than liabilities with ample stockholder's equity) yet is not liquid. This situation can occur when a business mismanages its cash resources which come under stress (as it possibly overinvested in fixed assets and is running short on cash to pay current bills). The financial ratio analyses provided address both solvency and liquidity issues for our fictitious company.

Current ratio

The *current ratio* tests the short-term liability-paying ability of a business. It is calculated by dividing total current assets by total current liabilities in a company's most recent balance sheet. The current ratio for the company is computed as follows:

Current Ratio, FYE:	**12/31/2019**	**12/31/2020**
Total Current Assets	$13,053,000	$20,602,000
Total Current Liabilities	$5,958,000	$9,961,750
Current Ratio	2.19	2.07

The current ratio is hardly ever expressed as a percent (which would be 207% for our example company for FYE 12/31/20). The current ratio for the business is stated as 2.07 to 1.00, or more simply just as 2.07.

The common opinion is that the current ratio for a business should be 2 to 1 or higher (although this depends on the type of industry the company operates within as in some instances, current ratios closer to 1.25 to 1.00 are acceptable). Most businesses find that their creditors expect this minimum current ratio. In other words, short-term creditors generally like to see a business limit its current liabilities to one-half or less of its current assets.

Why do short-term creditors put this limit on a business? The main reason is to provide a safety cushion of protection for the payment of the company's short-term liabilities. A current ratio of 2 to 1 means there is $2 of cash and current assets that should be converted into cash during the near future that will be available to pay each $1 of current liabilities that come due in roughly the same time period. Each dollar of short-term liabilities is backed up with $2 of cash on hand or near-term cash inflows. The extra dollar of current assets provides a margin of safety for the creditors.

A company may be able to pay its liabilities on time with a current ratio of less than 2 to 1, or perhaps even if its current ratio were as low as 1 to 1. In our business example, the company has borrowed $2 million using short-term notes payable, which equals 9.7% of its total current assets. In this situation, the company's lenders would probably be willing to provide additional short-term loans to the business given its solid current ratio, relatively low short-term borrowing ratio to current assets (of 9.7%), and its solid profitability (in 2020).

Net working capital

We would also like to note that the company's net working capital (defined as total current assets less total current liabilities) amounts to approximately $10.6 million as of FYE 12/31/20. The reason we have presented net working capital right after the current ratio is that lenders often incorporate loan covenants that state a business must maintain net working capital of X millions of dollars (to ensure ample internal liquidity is maintained).

Net Working Capital, FYE:	12/31/2019	12/31/2020
Total Current Assets	$13,053,000	$20,602,000
Total Current Liabilities	$5,958,000	$9,961,750
Net Working Capital	$7,095,000	$10,640,250

In summary, short-term sources of credit generally like to see a company's current assets be double its current liabilities (again, depending on the industry) along with maintaining strong levels of net working capital. After all, creditors are not owners – they do not share in the profit earned by the business. The income on their loans is limited to the interest they charge (and collect). As creditors, they quite properly minimize their loan risks; as limited-income (fixed-income) investors, they are not compensated to take on much risk.

Acid test ratio (aka quick ratio)

Inventory generally is many weeks or months away from conversion into cash. Products are typically held two, three, or four months before being sold. If sales are made on credit, which is normal when one business sells to another business (i.e., a B-to-B business model), there is a second waiting period before the receivables are collected. In short, inventory is not nearly as liquid as accounts receivable; it takes much longer to convert inventory first into sales and then into cash. Furthermore, there is no guarantee that all the products in inventory will be sold, as inventory can become obsolete, spoiled, lost/stolen, and so on.

A more severe measure of the short-term liability-paying ability of a business is the *acid test ratio* (aka *quick ratio*), which excludes inventory (and prepaid expenses). Only cash, short-term marketable securities investments (if any), and accounts receivable are counted as sources to pay the current liabilities of the business.

This ratio is also called the quick ratio because only cash and assets quickly convertible into cash are included in the amount available for paying current liabilities; it is more in the nature of a liquidity ratio that focuses on how much cash and near-cash assets a business possesses to pay its short-term liabilities.

In this example, the company's acid test ratio is calculated as follows (the business has no investments in marketable securities):

Quick or Acid Test Ratio, FYE:	12/31/2019	12/31/2020
Total Current Assets	$13,053,000	$20,602,000
Less: Inventory & Other Current Assets	($4,631,000)	($2,166,000)
Net Current Assets	$8,422,000	$18,436,000
Current Liabilities	$5,958,000	$9,961,750
Quick or Acid Test Ratio	1.41	1.85

The general rule is that a company's acid test ratio should be 1 to 1 or better, although there are many exceptions. You may also note that while the company's current ratio decreased from 2.19 for FYE 12/31/19 to 2.07 for FYE 12/31/20, its quick ratio actually increased from 1.41 to 1.85 (an improvement). You may ask how this happened and the answer is simple. The company is shedding its old technology product business and is reducing its investment in inventory as a result.

Debt-to-equity ratio

Some debt is generally good, but too much debt is dangerous. The *debt-to-equity ratio* is an indicator of whether a company is using debt prudently, or perhaps has gone too far and is overburdened with debt that may cause problems. For this example, the company's debt-to-equity ratio calculation is:

Debt to Equity Ratio, FYE:	12/31/2019	12/31/2020
Total Liabilities	$8,458,000	$16,586,750
Total Owner's Equity	$11,630,714	$21,904,536
Debt-to-Equity Ratio	0.73	0.76

This ratio tells us that the company is using $0.76 of liabilities in addition to each $1 of stockholders' equity in the business. Notice that all liabilities (non-interest-bearing as well as interest-bearing, and both short-term and long-term) are included in this ratio, and that all owners' equity (invested capital stock and retained earnings) is included.

This business, with its .76 debt-to-equity ratio, would be viewed as moderately leveraged. *Leverage* refers to using the equity capital base to raise additional capital from nonowner sources. In other words, the business is using $1.76 of total capital for every $1 of equity capital.

Historically, most businesses have tended to stay below a 1-to-1 debt-to-equity ratio. They don't want to take on too much debt, or they cannot convince lenders to put up more than one-half of their assets. However, some capital-intensive (asset-heavy) businesses such as public utilities and financial institutions operate with debt-to-equity ratios much higher than 1 to 1. In other words, they are highly leveraged.

But a word of caution in today's world (which we address more fully in Chapter 12 on financial engineering): Over the decade since the Great Recession of 2007 through 2009, the world has been flooded with massive cash infusions from global central banks with undertaking highly accommodative monetary policies, including driving interest rates down. By some estimates, over \$20 trillion of cash/currency has been injected into the global economy by the world's leading central banks, which was amplified by the global COVID-19 pandemic starting in 2020. This has resulted in a drastic decline in interest rates that, unbelievable as it may sound, has resulted in over \$15 trillion of global debt generating negative interest rates (yes, you heard us right).

 These policy changes have encouraged businesses to secure new and unbelievably cheap debt to be used for business purposes ranging from investing in capital equipment to repurchasing its issued shares, helping drive up EPS (see below). This so-called "easy" monetary environment has unfortunately also produced two unwanted side effects:

1. Debt-to-equity ratio historical "norms" (for lack of a better term) of, let's say, less than 1 to 1 (as previously noted) have been sacrificed in the name of cheap (i.e., low interest rates), abundant (i.e., large amounts of fresh/new capital), and easy (i.e., limited financial performance covenant requirements) debt. So not only are companies becoming more and more leveraged, the quality of the debt, via establishing performance covenants to ensure that a company's performance is acceptable, is being reduced or in some cases eliminated. It doesn't take a genius to quickly conclude that a more leveraged company with lower-quality debt is generally a recipe for disaster.

2. When companies use debt to repurchase their own shares (a very common practice over the past few years), the number of shares outstanding when calculating its EPS decreases (e.g., Company XYZ had 1 million shares outstanding and elected to repurchase 100,000, leaving 900,000 shares remaining as outstanding). With fewer outstanding shares and a relatively constant net profit, the company provides the appearance, or some may say illusion, that its EPS is increasing even though its net profit did not change. This concept is a perfect example of what is commonly referred to as financial engineering – a topic that we will dig into in Chapter 12 and is something that is extremely important to understand in today's world economy.

Debt-to-tangible net equity

This financial ratio analysis takes the debt-to-net-worth analysis one step further by extracting intangible assets from the calculation. Intangible assets represent a broad range of assets, including software development costs, capitalized intellectual property (e.g., patents), content creation, acquisition goodwill, and similar types of assets that are not tangible in nature. The reason this calculation is important to lenders is that in today's rapidly moving economy, especially for technology-based companies, what may be of value today could be completely worthless in two years. Thus, by stripping out the intangible assets from the debt-to-equity ratio, a lender has a better view of a company's real financial leverage.

The debt-to-tangible net equity for our sample company tells an interesting story as follows:

Debt to Tangible Net Equity Ratio, FYE:	12/31/2019	12/31/2020
Total Liabilities	$8,458,000	$16,586,750
Total Owner's Equity	$11,630,714	$21,904,536
Less: Intangible Assets	($1,000,000)	($12,500,000)
Tangible Net Equity	$10,630,714	$9,404,536
Debt to Tangible Net Equity Ratio	0.80	1.76

You can see the substantial increase in the company's leverage from FYE 12/31/19 of .80 to 1.76 for FYE 12/31/20 (doubling in one year). The reason for this increase is centered in the fact that the company raised a large amount of capital during FYE 12/31/20 for an asset acquisition that resulted in an investment of $12.5 in intangible assets (for goodwill, rights to intellectual property, etc.). Based on FYE 12/31/20 operating results compared to the prior year, it looks like the company made a prudent investment (given the substantial increase in net profits from 2020 compared to 2019). Will this hold in the future? Well, only time will tell but the debt-to-tangible net equity ratio can help identify potential additional financial leverage risk impacting this company (which lenders will want to be well aware of).

BENCHMARK FINANCIAL RATIOS – FINANCIAL PERFORMANCE
Return on sales (ROS)

Generating sales while controlling expenses is how a business makes profit. The profit residual slice of a company's total sales revenue pie is expressed by the *return on sales ratio*, which is profit divided by sales revenue for the period. The company's return on sales ratio for its latest two years is:

Return on Sales, FYE:	12/31/2019	12/31/2020
Net Income (Loss)	($248,286)	$2,913,821
Revenue, Net	$53,747,000	$72,198,250
Return on Sales	-0.46%	4.04%

There is another way of explaining the return on sales ratio. For FYE 12/31/20, each $100 of sales revenue the business earned generated $4.04 of net income and expenses of $95.96. Return on sales varies quite markedly from one industry to another. Some businesses do well with only a 2–4% return on sales; others need more than 20% to justify the large amount of capital invested in their assets. For a company operating in the technology market, especially with a focus on software, return on sales far north of 10% is now the norm (so this company appears to be underperforming compared to its peers).

Return on equity (ROE)

Owners take the risk of whether their business can earn a profit and sustain its profit performance over the years. How much would you pay for a business that consistently suffers a loss? The value of the owners' investment depends first and foremost on the past and potential future profit performance of the business – or not just profit, we should say, but profit relative to the capital invested to earn that profit.

For instance, suppose a business earns $100,000 annual net income for its stockholders. If its stockholders' equity is $250,000, then its profit performance relative to the stockholders' capital used to make that profit is 40%, which is very good indeed. If, however, stockholders' equity is $2,500,000, then the company's profit performance equals only 4% of owners' equity, which is weak relative to the owners' capital used to earn that profit.

In short, profit should be compared with the amount of capital invested to earn that profit. Profit for a period divided by the amount of capital invested to earn that profit is generally called *return on investment* (ROI). ROI is a broad concept that applies to almost any sort of investment of capital.

The owners' historical investment in a business is the total of the owners' equity accounts in the company's balance sheet. Their profit is bottom-line net income for the period – well, maybe not all of net income. A business corporation may issue *preferred stock*, on which a fixed amount of dividends has to be paid each year. The preferred stock shares have the first claim on dividends from net income. Therefore, preferred stock dividends are subtracted from net income to determine the *net income available for the common stockholders*. Our company has issued preferred stock, so not all net income "belongs" to its common stockholders. However, for simplicity in displaying this calculation, we will assume that all the net income earned by the company is available to all the equity owners (both common and preferred).

Dividing annual net income by stockholders' equity gives the *return on equity* (ROE) ratio. The calculation for the company's ROE in this example is:

Return on Owner's Equity, FYE:	12/31/2019	12/31/2020
End-of-Year Total Owner's Equity	$11,630,714	$21,904,536
Net Income (Loss)	($248,286)	$2,913,821
Return on Average Owner's Equity	-2.13%	13.30%

Note: We use the ending balance of stockholders' equity to simplify the calculation. Alternatively, the weighted average during the year could be used, and should be if there have been significant changes during the year.

By most standards, this company's 13.30% annual ROE for FYE 12/31/20 would be acceptable but not impressive. However, everything is relative. ROE should be compared with industrywide averages and with investment alternatives. Also, the risk factor is important: Just how risky is the stockholders' capital investment in the business?

We need to know much more about the history and prospects of the business to reach a conclusion regarding whether its 13.30% ROE is good, mediocre, or poor. Also, we should consider the *opportunity cost of capital* – that is, the ROI the stockholders could have earned on the next-best use of their capital. Furthermore, we have not considered the personal income tax on dividends paid to its individual stockholders. In summary, judging ROE is not a simple matter!

Return on assets (ROA)

Here is another useful profit performance ratio:

Return on Assets, FYE:	12/31/2019	12/31/2020
End-of-Year Total Assets	$20,088,714	$38,491,286
Net Income (Loss) Before Interest & Income Taxes	($231,286)	$4,882,821
Return on Average Assets	-1.15%	12.69%

The *return on assets* (ROA) ratio for the FYE 12/31/20 reveals that the business earned $12.69 before interest and income tax expenses on each $100 of assets. The ROA is compared with the annual interest rate on the company's borrowed money. In this example, the company's annual interest rate on its short-term and long-term debt is approximately 5.0%. The business earned 12.69% on the money borrowed, as measured by the ROA. The difference or spread between the two rates is a favorable spread equal to 7.69 percentage points, which increases the earnings after interest for stockholders. This source of profit enhancement is called *financial leverage gain*. In contrast, if a company's ROA is less than its interest rate, it suffers a financial leverage loss.

CHAPTER 9

Advanced Financial Ratio Analysis and Terminology

PURPOSE AND ADVANCED TERMINOLOGY

This chapter picks up on our fictitious company overviewed in Chapter 8 and pushes forward with more advanced financial ratio and business analysis tools. We should note that it would be impossible to cover the entire range of financial tools, analyses, ratios, and so on utilized by professionals today, as just about everyone seems to have a new and wonderful analysis available to impress the powers that be. Our goal in this chapter is to provide more depth and understanding of various financial analyses that are commonly referenced and used in today's business world. You will notice a bias toward (a) analyzing cash flows and (b) more subjective calculations or estimates of figures, as when different people with different levels of training and expertise get involved, you are bound to get different perspectives (which of course is par for the course in the financial world these days).

We make every effort to provide some level of consistency and simplicity with the concepts covered in this chapter, but this would be a good point in the book to remind yourself to slow down and, if necessary, read the material multiple times. Before we start the discussion, a list of more advanced financial and accounting terminology has been provided to really help improve your financial vocabulary.

➢ EBITDA: This is one of the most used (and abused) terms in finance today and stands for earnings before interest, taxes, depreciation, and amortization. A shorter version that is also used frequently is EBIT or earnings before interest and taxes. The reason for EBITDA's popularity is that capital sources want to clearly understand just how much earnings a company can generate in the form of operating cash on a periodic basis. EBITDA strips out interest, taxes, and depreciation and amortization expense (both noncash expenses) to calculate what is perceived to be a company's ability to generate internal positive cash flow (which is widely used when evaluating the value of a company and its ability to service debt).

➢ Free Cash Flow: FCF is closely related to EBITDA but takes into consideration numerous other factors or adjustments such as the need for a company to invest in equipment or intangible assets on a periodic basis (to remain competitive), the required or set debt service the company is obligated to pay each year (for interest and principal payments), any guaranteed returns on preferred equity, and other similar adjustments. FCF can be a highly subjective calculation based on the estimates and definitions used by different parties.

➢ YOY and CAGR: YOY stands for a year-over-year change in a financial performance (e.g., sales change for the current 12-month period compared to the prior 12-month period). CAGR stands for compounded annual growth rate and represents a financial calculation that evaluates a financial performance over a number of periods (e.g., sales increased at a CAGR of 15.5% for the five-year period of 2016 through 2020).

➢ Sustainable Growth Rate: This calculation estimates a company's maximum growth rate it can achieve by using internal operating capital (i.e., positive cash flow) only. When a company exceeds its sustainable growth rate, external capital such as loans or equity from new investors may need to be secured to support ongoing operations.

➢ Debt Service: Total debt service includes both required loan interest and principal payments due over a period of time.

➢ B2B and B2C: A company that sells primarily to other businesses is B2B (business-to-business), whereas a company that sells primarily to consumers is B2C (business to consumer).

- Burn Rate and the Runway: A burn rate is generally used for newer businesses or starts-up that have not achieved profitability and are "burning" a large amount of cash. The burn rate calculates the amount of cash burn a company is incurring over a specific period, such as a month or a quarter. If a company has a burn rate of $250,000 a month (before generating any sales), then an investor could quickly calculate that this company would need $3 million of capital to support it for one year. The runway calculates how much time a company has before it runs out of cash. In our example, if the company has $1 million of cash left and is burning $250,000 per month, it has a remaining runway of four months.

➤ TTM and FTM: TTM stands for trailing twelve months and FTM stands for forward twelve months. These figures are often used by parties to help understand a company's annual operating results that are not in sync with its FYE (e.g., how much sales revenue was generated for the period of QE 9/30/19 through QE 6/30/20, 12 months of operating history). TTM and FTM can be especially useful when evaluating companies that are growing rapidly or have experienced a recent significant change in business.

Throughout the remainder of this book, we will reference these concepts more frequently so you may want to bookmark this section to help refresh your memory.

A new financial statement

To start, Exhibit 9.1 introduces a new financial statement, the *statement of changes in stockholders' equity for year*, that we have not presented before in the book. In some respects, this is not really a financial statement as it is more of a supporting schedule that summarizes changes in the stockholders' equity accounts.

EXHIBIT 9.1 Unaudited Statement of Changes in Stockholders' Equity

Unaudited - Prepared by Company Management

QW Example Tech., Inc.
Unaudited Financial Statements
Statement of Changes in Stockholder's Equity
For the Fiscal Year Ending 12/31/2020

Description	Common Shares	Common Amount	Preferred Shares	Preferred Amount	Retained Earnings	Total
Balance, January 1, 2020	1,000,000	$10,000,000	0	$0	$1,630,714	$11,630,714
Sale of Preferred Stock (convertible into common)			500,000	$8,000,000		$8,000,000
Net Income					$2,913,821	$2,913,821
Dividends					($640,000)	($640,000)
Other Accumulated Income (Expenses)					$0	$0
Balance, December 31, 2020	1,000,000	$10,000,000	500,000	$8,000,000	$3,904,536	$21,904,536
Fully Diluted Shares:						
Common	1,000,000					
Preferred	500,000					
Stock Option Grants	125,000					
Total	1,625,000					

Note: The company has issued an outstanding 125,000 employee stock option grants as of 12/31/20.

Confidential - Property of QW Example Tech., Inc.

The business issued 500,000 additional shares of preferred capital stock during the year for $8,000,000 to help finance an acquisition. The $8,000,0000 cash from issuing the shares are reported in the statement of changes in stockholders' equity as well as the statement of cash flows (see Exhibit 1.3). Net income for the year is reported as an increase in retained earnings, and cash dividends paid to stockholders as a decrease.

The statement of changes in stockholders' equity is definitely needed when a business has a capitalization (ownership) structure that includes two or more classes of stock (which is the case with our sample company), and when a business owns some of its own capital stock shares (called *treasury stock*). This financial statement is also needed when a business has recorded certain types of losses and gains that bypass the income statement. The amounts of any such special gains and losses are recorded in a special stockholders' equity account called *Accumulated Other Comprehensive Income*.

The term *comprehensive income* connotes that, in addition to net income that flows through the income statement into the retained earnings account, additional gains and losses have been recorded that have not been reported in the income statement. The accumulated other comprehensive income account serves like a second retained earnings type of account, which holds the cumulative result of recording certain types of gains and losses. Exploring these special gains and losses would take us into a technical territory beyond the scope of this book.

The statement of changes in stockholders' equity can be complex and highly technical but does provide valuable information related to the total shares issued and outstanding as well as the type of equity (preferred versus common).

ADVANCED BENCHMARK FINANCIAL RATIOS AND CONCEPTS
Earnings per share (EPS)

In contrast to the ratios discussed in Chapter 8 (which are calculated independently of the financial statements), the earnings per share (EPS) ratio is reported at the bottom of the income statements prepared and issued by public companies. You do not have to calculate it but given its importance you should surely understand how it is determined. Private companies are not required to report EPS, but many larger, more sophisticated private companies do report this figure (which is the case with our sample company).

However, as a stockholder of a private company you may find it helpful to calculate its EPS.

The capital stock shares of approximately 6,000 domestic business corporations are traded in public markets – the New York Stock Exchange, Nasdaq, and electronic stock exchanges. The day-to-day, even minute-by-minute, market price changes of these shares receive a great deal of attention. More than any other single factor, the market value of capital stock shares depends on the past and forecast net income (earnings) of a business.

Suppose we tell you that the market price of a stock is $48 and ask you whether this value is too high or too low, or just about right. You could compare the market price with the stockholders' equity per share reported in the balance sheet, called the *book value per share*, which is about $15 in our example – $22.5 million of net shareholders' equity divided by 1,500,000 of total outstanding common and preferred shares. (Recall that a company's total assets minus its total liabilities equal its stockholders' equity.) The book value method has a respectable history in securities analysis. Today, however, the book value approach plays second fiddle to the earnings-based approach. The starting point is to calculate earnings (on net income) per share.

One of the most widely used ratios in investment analysis is *earnings per share* (EPS). The essential calculation of basic earnings per share is as follows for our company example:

Earnings per Share Basic, FYE:	12/31/2019	12/31/2020
Net Profit (Loss)	($248,286)	$2,913,821
Less: Preferred Dividends	$0	($640,000)
Earnings Available for Common	($248,286)	$2,273,821
Shares Outstanding, Basic	1,000,000	1,000,000
Earnings per Share, Basic	($0.25)	$2.91

Note: To be technically accurate, the weighted average number of all equivalent common shares outstanding during the year should be used – based on the actual number of shares outstanding each month (or day) during the period.

First off, notice that the numerator (the top number) in the EPS ratio is *net income available for common stockholders*, which equals bottom-line net income less any dividends paid to the preferred stockholders of the business. Many business corporations issue preferred stock that requires a fixed amount of dividends to be paid each year. The mandatory annual dividends to the preferred stockholders are deducted from net income to determine the net income available for the common stockholders.

Second, please notice the word *basic* in front of *earnings per share*, which means that the actual number of common stock shares in the hands of stockholders is the denominator (the bottom number) in the EPS calculation. Many businesses have entered contracts of one sort or another that require the company at some time in the future to issue additional stock shares at prices below the market value of the stock shares at that time. The shares under these contracts have not been actually issued yet but probably will be in the future.

For example, business corporations award managers *stock options* to buy common stock shares of the company at fixed prices (generally equal to the present market price or current value of the shares). If in the future the market value of the shares rises over the fixed option prices, the managers will exercise their rights and buy capital stock shares at a bargain price. With stock options, therefore, the number of stock shares is subject to inflation. When (and if) the additional shares are issued, EPS will suffer because net income will have to be spread over a larger number of stock shares. EPS will be diluted, or thinned down, because of the larger denominator in the EPS ratio.

Basic EPS does not recognize the additional shares that will be issued when stock options are exercised. Also, basic EPS does not take into account potential dilution effects of any convertible bonds and convertible preferred stock that have been issued by a business. These securities can be converted at the option of the security holders into common stock shares at predetermined prices.

To warn investors of the potential effects of stock options and convertible securities, a second EPS is reported by public corporations, called fully *diluted* EPS. This lower EPS takes into account the potential dilution effects caused by issuing additional common stock shares under stock option plans, convertible securities, and any other commitments a business has entered into that could require it to issue additional stock shares at predetermined prices in the future. For our sample company, we have included a calculation of fully diluted EPS:

Earnings per Share Fully Diluted, FYE:	12/31/2019	12/31/2020
Net Profit (Loss)	($248,286)	$2,913,821
Shares Outstanding, Fully Diluted (#)	1,000,000	1,625,000
Earnings per Share, Fully Diluted	($0.25)	$1.79

Upon reviewing the fully diluted EPS calculation, you can see that for FYE 12/31/20, the figure is much lower than the basic EPS even though 100% of the net profit is used in the calculation (as it is assumed in a fully diluted calculation that all profits are available to all company shares, which are treated equally). This is why understanding the fully diluted EPS is so important; in a sense, it calculates the available earnings per share in a "worst"-case scenario assuming earnings must be spread out over the maximum number of outstanding shares.

Basic EPS and fully diluted EPS (if applicable) must be reported in the income statements of publicly owned corporations. This indicates the importance of EPS. In contrast, none of the other ratios discussed in Chapter 8 or this chapter must be reported, although many public companies report selected ratios.

Price/earnings (P/E) ratio

The market price of stock shares of a public business corporation is compared with its EPS and expressed in the *price/earnings (P/E) ratio* as follows:

Price-to-Earnings Ratio, FYE:	12/31/2019	12/31/2020
Market Value per Share (*)	$16.00	$42.00
Earnings per Share, Fully Diluted	($0.25)	$1.79
Price-to-Earnings Ratio	n/a	23.42
* Assumed price of company shares as quoted per a public stock market (e.g., NYSE)		

For our sample company, suppose a public market quotes the current stock price at $42 per share and its fully diluted EPS for the most recent FYE 12/31/20 is $1.79. Thus, its P/E ratio is 23.42. Like other ratios discussed in this chapter, the P/E ratio should be compared with industry- and market-wide averages to judge whether it is acceptable, too high, or too low. At one time a P/E ratio of 8 to 12 was considered reasonable. As we write this sentence, P/E ratios north of 20 are not only considered acceptable but in today's market, might be viewed as low for a rapidly growing technology company.

Now, here is a problem in calculating the P/E ratio for a public company: Should you use its *basic* EPS or its fully *diluted* EPS? If the business reports only basic EPS, there is no problem. But when a public company reports both, which EPS should you use? Well, it is done both ways. Our advice is to check the legend in the stock market tables in the *Wall Street Journal* and the *New York Times* to find out which EPS the newspaper uses in reporting the P/E ratios for companies. Using fully diluted EPS is more conservative; that is, it gives a higher P/E ratio.

The market prices for stock shares of a private business are not available to the public at large. Private company shares are usually not actively traded but when they are traded, the price per share is not made public. Nevertheless, stockholders in these businesses are interested in what their shares are worth. To estimate the value of stock shares a P/E multiple can be used. In the company sample, its fully diluted EPS is $1.79 for the most recent year (see the previous calculation). Suppose you own some of the capital stock shares, and someone offers to buy your shares. You could establish an offer price at, say, 18 times basic EPS. This would be $32.22 per share. The potential buyer may not be willing to pay this price, or he or she might be willing to pay even more (if they are very bullish on the company's growth prospects).

Market cap

The market cap is the total market capitalization or public value of a company. For example, suppose the stock shares of a public company are currently trading at $65 per share, and the business has 100 million shares outstanding. The *market cap*, or total market value capitalization of the company, is $6.5 billion ($65 market value per share × 100 million capital stock shares = $6.5 billion). We'd bet you dollars to doughnuts that if you compared the market cap of most businesses with the shareholders' equity amounts reported in their latest balance sheets, the market caps would be considerably higher and perhaps much higher.

The book value (balance sheet value) of shareholders' equity is the historical record of the amounts invested in the business by the owners in the past plus its retained earnings accumulated over the years. Over time these amounts become more and more out of date. In contrast, the market cap is based on the current market value of the company's stock shares. If a business gets into financial straits, its market cap may drop below the book value of its owners' equity – at least for the time being. In rare cases a company's cash balance may be more than its market cap.

Debt service coverage ratio

Thus far, the ratios provided and associated analyses have tended to focus on the income statement and balance sheet (ignoring the cash flow statement). This is traditionally where most parties focus their attention, as the information gleaned from the calculations is especially useful. But cash flow ratios and analyses are just as informative and in today's world have become mainstays when evaluating a company's operating performance and financial viability. Here we present two cash flow–based ratios and analysis tools that are widely used in the market, starting with the debt service coverage ratio.

The goal with this ratio is to ensure that the company can not only cover its interest expense but in addition make all necessary debt principal payments as well. For our sample company, here is the calculation:

Debt Service Coverage Ratio, FYE:	12/31/2019	12/31/2020
Net Income (Loss)	($248,286)	$2,913,821
Interest Expense	$150,000	$400,000
Depreciation & Amortization Expense	$1,814,286	$2,421,429
Adjusted Debt Service Cash Flow	$1,716,000	$5,735,250
Interest Expense	$150,000	$400,000
Loan Principal Payments Due, 1 Yr.	$1,000,000	$2,000,000
Total Debt Service Payments, 1 Yr.	$1,150,000	$2,400,000
Debt Service Coverage Ratio	1.49	2.39

It goes without saying that this ratio needs to be north of 1.00 to 1.00 with most lenders demanding a minimum ratio of at least 1.50 to 1.00 (and often higher) to ensure there is a cushion available to cover any potential cash flow problems or hiccups. So, the good news for our example company for FYE 12/31/20 is that their 2.39 DSCR is well above the target of 1.50 – but it does highlight the importance of managing available cash flow in relation to both total interest expense and debt principal payments due.

You will also note that no adjustment has been made for the $640,000 of annual preferred stock dividends. The reason is that the company's lenders sit in a senior position to the preferred stockholders and are most interested in the company being able to cover the total debt service prior to any preferred stock dividends. In fact, experienced lenders will often incorporate a covenant in the loan agreement that states that preferred dividends cannot be paid unless the DSCR is above 2.00.

Adjusted EBITDA

To refresh your memory, EBITDA stands for earnings before interest, taxes, depreciation, and amortization expense and usually is not separately disclosed in a company's financial report (so it must be calculated, which we have done below). Adjusted EBITDA is calculated by increasing or decreasing EBITDA for expenses or charges that are considered nonrecurring or one-time in nature and then decreasing EBITDA for normal and customary capital expenditures that must be incurred to ensure continued operating performance levels. For example, a manufacturing company must constantly invest in new equipment to support business operations (as the old equipment becomes obsolete and/or is worn out through depreciation). In our sample company, adjusted EBITDA is calculated as follows:

Adjusted EBITDA, FYE:	12/31/2019	12/31/2020
Net Income (Loss)	($248,286)	$2,913,821
Addback:		
Interest	$150,000	$400,000
Taxes	($133,000)	$1,569,000
Depreciation & Amortization	$1,814,286	$2,421,429
EBITDA	$1,583,000	$7,304,250
Adjustments:		
Normal & Recurring Fixed Asset Add.	($460,000)	($497,500)
Normal & Recurring Intangible Asset Add.	($250,000)	($3,125,000)
Other/Nonrecurring Expenses	$250,000	$2,000,000
Total Adjustments	($460,000)	($1,622,500)
Adjusted EBITDA	$1,123,000	$5,681,750

The party calculating adjusted EBITDA in this situation (e.g., an external analyst or an internal member of the management team) has determined that the company will need to invest approximately $3.6 million a year ($497,500 plus $3,125,000) in fixed and intangible assets to remain competitive. Please note that this figure represents an estimate or possibly nothing more than a SWAG (scientific wild-ass guess; see Chapter 10) but the point is, almost all businesses need to invest in fixed assets on an annual basis to remain viable (the reason depreciation and amortization expense is recorded, as fixed assets, tangible or intangible, generally lose value over time).

In addition, the party allowed for the add-back of other expenses that were assumed to be one-time events (and not likely to recur in future years).

This produces an adjusted EBITDA of approximately $5.7 million for the company, which appears reasonable, but let us take the analysis one step further to compare the adjusted EBITDA against annual cash payment commitments to gain a clear picture as follows:

Adjusted EBITDA to Comm. Rate, FYE:	12/31/2019	12/31/2020
Adjusted EBITDA	$1,123,000	$5,681,750
Annual Cash Payment Commitments:		
Income Tax Expense	($133,000)	$1,569,000
Debt Service (principal & interest)	$1,150,000	$2,400,000
Preferred Dividend	$0	$640,000
Total Annual Cash Payment Comm.	$1,017,000	$4,609,000
Adjusted EBITDA Cash Coverage Ratio	1.10	1.23

So, the real question with this calculation is, does this indicate a problem? For FYE 12/31/20, the company did generate enough adjusted internal cash flow to cover all expenses, support normalized capital expenditures (remember, an estimate), meet total debt service commitments, pay the preferred stock dividend, and make sure the government's tax obligation was paid. However, the coverage ratio of 1.23 is a little "thin," as there is not much room for error with the operating results, so for our sample company, this is a trend worth keeping your eye on as it may warrant taking a deeper dive into the company's financial reports and its plans to gain additional clarification on any potential liquidity issues or problems that might be coming down the road.

Loan-to-value ratio

One final ratio we want to cover in this chapter is what is commonly referred to as the LTV or loan-to-value ratio. This ratio compares the total value of an asset or an entire company against the total amount of outstanding debt (that is secured by the asset or company). In our sample company, for FYE 12/31/20 the total outstanding loans secured by company assets amounts to $8 million ($2 million of current debt and $6 million of long-term debt). Per the figures provided previously in this chapter, the total fair value of the company as established by public markets is estimated to be approximately $68 million ($42 current price per share multiplied by 1,625,000 fully diluted outstanding shares). So, in this case, the LTV ratio is roughly 11.8% ($8 million divided by $68 million), an extremely comfortable level.

You will find that the LTV ratio is more commonly used in businesses operating in real estate, mineral extraction (e.g., the oil and gas industry), and similar companies that require extremely large capital investments in fixed assets. The reason for this is that the capital sources required to support these investments is usually heavily dependent on debt (from banks or other lending sources). Lenders not only want to make sure that a borrower has more than enough resources to cover annual debt service commitments (i.e., the loan can be repaid from internal cash flows), but in addition, if the borrower defaults on the loan, the lender wants to feel comfortable that the value of the asset or property is always greater than the loan (so if it is forced to foreclose on the loan and take title to and sell the asset, the lender can realize enough funds to cover the loan).

While there are no set rules, lenders generally like to keep LTV ratios under 70% and preferably lower. This provides a reasonable cushion in case a fire sale of an asset or property occurs that results in a lower value being realized. Although an extreme example, anyone who lived through the Great Recession and housing market meltdown from 2007 through 2010 got a firsthand look at just how important LTV ratios were for the residential real estate industry.

A FINAL PIECE OF ADVICE

Countless other financial analyses and ratios can be derived from the financial information provided in financial statements and financial reports.

There is really no end to the financial analyses and ratios that can be calculated, so the trick is to focus on those financial analyses and ratios that have the most interpretive value for the user, and that are most relevant within an industry (for comparison purposes).

For the newbie, it is not easy to figure out which ratios are the most important. On the other hand, professional investors seem to use too many ratios rather than too few (and overcomplicate the analysis), in our opinion. Finding just the right balance is the key as you never know which ratio might provide a valuable clue to a stock's future market value direction.

CHAPTER 10

Projections and Forecasts – Living, Rolling, and Breathing

THE IMPORTANCE OF BUSINESS FORECAST MODELS

In Chapter 13, we introduce you to the importance and concept of business planning, and its role in determining how to capitalize a business. The planning process includes numerous elements ranging from assessing current market conditions to understanding the macroeconomic environment to evaluating personnel resources to preparing budgets, forecasts, and/or projections. This chapter focuses on one of the most critical elements of the planning process – preparing a forecast. For the balance of this chapter, the term *forecasts* will be used for consistency purposes, but it should be noted that businesses often utilize other terms, including *budgets* or *budgeting*, *projections*, and *proformas* (which basically all mean the same thing). We prefer to use the term *forecasts* as it is broader in scope and helps drive home a key concept related to building *top-down* forecast models (which we cover in this chapter).

Before we delve too deeply into the forecasting process, we make a quick attempt to properly define a forecast. Forecasts *are not* based on the concept of "How much can I spend in my division this year?" Rather, forecasts are more comprehensive in nature and are designed to capture all relevant

117

and critical financial data, including revenue levels, costs of sales, operating expenses, fixed asset expenditures, capital requirements, and the like. All too often, forecasts are associated with expense levels and management, which represent just one element of the entire forecasts.

Further, the forecasting process does not represent a chicken-and-egg riddle. From a financial perspective, the preparation of forecasts represents the end result of the entire planning process. Hence, you must first accumulate the necessary data and information on which to build a forecasting model prior to producing projected financial information (for an entire company or a specific division). There is no point in preparing a forecast that does not capture the real economic structure and viability of an entire entity or operating division.

We would also like to drive home once again the importance of preparing complete financial information within the financial forecasts. All too often, companies prepare financial forecasts focused on just the income statement and downplay the importance of the balance sheet and statement of cash flows (which may get put on the back burner). The importance of preparing complete financial forecasts will be on full display in this chapter, as we include forecasts for both the balance sheet and statement of cash flows.

The bottom line with forecasting (and the entire planning process) is that without having clearly identified business financial and performance objectives, the business is operating blind. Or, put simply, it would be like flying a plane without having a destination. The need for having clearly identified benchmarks and a roadmap to reach the benchmarks is essential for every business, regardless of size, shape, or form, as often the most important question of all comes down to this: "How am I doing against the plan?"

MANAGING THE FORECASTING PROCESS

Years ago, businesses tended to manage the forecasting process on an annual or maybe semiannual basis. The standard cycle started toward the end of each current FYE (maybe 30 to 90 days prior) as management would get the annual "budgeting" process fired up to plan for the upcoming year. We have no doubt that this annual forecasting process still occurs and is widely used but based on the economic realities of today's capitalist markets, the forecasting process must be managed as a living, breathing function that should be constantly updated as frequently as critical business information emerges, evolves, and/or changes.

 This does not mean that preparing updated forecasts needs to be completed weekly (which would be overkill), but trust us when we say that developing forecasting models that have the flexibility to always be rolled forward to look out 12 to 24 months from the end of any desired reporting period is now standard practice. This is not merely a nice-to-have; it but is now a must-have.

Understanding that the forecasting process represents a living, breathing function that requires proactive management on a monthly basis, we now turn our attention to some basic concepts to assist with preparing forecasts.

➤ *Initial Forecast, New Business:* For businesses or professionals that have already prepared prior-year forecasts, this bullet point may not be all that relevant. For first-timers preparing a forecast for a new business, you will want to become familiar with three acronyms: BOTE, WAG, and SWAG. These stand for back-of-the-envelope, wild-ass guess, and scientific wild-ass guess. You might notice a little humor when referring to these acronyms, but we are being quite serious. The forecasting process needs to start somewhere and often resides with executive management team members discussing a business idea or opportunity, jotting down some thoughts and basic numbers on the back of a napkin or envelope. This may then evolve into a wild-ass guess where an actual (albeit quite simple) preliminary forecast is prepared using a standard technology tool such as Microsoft Excel. Then, as additional information is obtained and incorporated into the forecast model, it transforms into a scientific wild-ass guess (where key data points and assumptions can be documented and defended). You would be amazed at how many businesses and forecasts get started with such a simple initial step, but you would be equally amazed at how quickly the forecast model evolves into a very sophisticated management tool.

➤ *Initial Forecast, Existing Business:* To start, you should have a solid understanding of your company's historical financial information and operating results. This history may stretch back three months, one year, five years, or longer, but the key concept is that having sound internal financial information represents an excellent place to start. However, remember that while the financial operating history of a company may provide a foundation on which to prepare a forecast, it by no means is an accurate or guaranteed predictor of future operating results. If the economic environment of a business has changed, then benchmarking off other similar businesses represents an effective means to build a reliable forecast.

➤ *Gather Reliable Data:* The availability of quality market, operational, and accounting/financial data represents the basis of the forecast. A good deal of this data often comes from internal sources. For example, when a sales region is preparing a budget for the upcoming year, the sales manager may survey the direct sales representatives on what they feel their customers will demand in terms of products and services in the coming year. With this information, you can determine sales volumes, personnel levels, wage rates, commission plans, and so on. While internal information is of value, it represents only half the battle because external information and data is just as critical to accumulate. Having access to quality and reliable external third-party information is essential to the overall business planning process and the production of reliable forecasts. Market forces and trends may be occurring that can impact your business over the next 24 months (that may not be reflected in the previous year's operating results).

➤ *Involve Key Team Members:* The forecasting process represents a critical function in most companies' accounting and financial department and rightfully so, as these are the people who understand the numbers the best. Although the financial and accounting types produce the final budget, they rely on data that comes from numerous parties such as marketing, manufacturing, and sales. You must ensure that all key management team members are involved in the forecasting process, covering all critical business functions, to produce a reliable projection. Just as you would not have a regional sales manager prepare a fixed asset schedule (tracking all asset additions, disposals, and depreciation expense), you would not have your accountant estimate sales volumes by product line during the holiday season (and what prices the products may fetch). Critical business data comes from numerous parties, all of which must be included in the forecasting process to produce the most reliable information possible.

➤ *Consistency and Completeness:* The financial forecasts prepared should be both complete and consistent to maximize their value. When we reference *complete*, we mean that all relevant financial information should be presented in the forecasts to ensure that the target audience has the proper output and data on which to base economic decisions. Consistency implies that the financial forecasts are prepared in a like format to the periodic financial information provided to the target audience (including all critical financial data points, KPIs, etc.). There is no benefit to preparing financial forecasts in a format that is different than the periodic internal financial information produced and delivered to the management team (you can imagine the confusion that would ensue). Financial forecast models should be designed to be in sync with critical reporting and utilize the same format for ease of understanding and decision-making.

➤ *Timing and Presentation:* As previously mentioned, the annual budgeting process is a thing of the past. While an annual forecast can be produced just prior to the beginning of a new FYE to start the process, management should be prepared, on at least a quarterly basis and for more fluid, high-paced businesses, monthly, to revise and update forecasts as business conditions change. Presentation-wise, generally the nearer the term covered by the forecasts the more detailed the information and frequency of reporting periods being prepared. If you are preparing a forecast for the coming fiscal year, the monthly financial information should be provided, but if you are looking out three to five years, then providing quarterly financial information should suffice (for years three through five).

If you did not notice, the concept of CART is alive and well and fully embedded in best-in-class business planning and forecasting functions. Companies need to develop and utilize financial forecasting models that are highly flexible and easily adaptable, to adjust to rapidly changing business conditions. In the following section, we provide additional insight on how you can develop more powerful forecasts.

INCREASING THE POWER AND VALUE OF YOUR FORECAST

We start this section noting that the list of concepts, strategies, and tools overviewed here is not meant to be all-inclusive but rather these have been selected to assist with making financial forecasts even more useful and powerful, starting with *SWOT*. This acronym stands for strengths, weaknesses, opportunities, and threats and is a business management assessment tool designed to assist the company's management team with preparing a qualitative assessment of the business, helping to keep all parties focused on key issues. The SWOT analysis is often incorporated into a company's planning function (discussed in Chapter 13) but can also be extremely helpful with preparing financial forecasts.

A SWOT analysis is usually broken down into a matrix of four segments. Two of the segments are geared toward positive attributes –strengths and opportunities – and two are geared toward negative attributes –weaknesses and threats. In addition, the analysis differentiates between internal company source attributes and external, or outside of the company, source attributes. Generally, the SWOT analysis is prepared by senior management team members to ensure that critical conditions are communicated to management for inclusion in the budget. If used correctly, a SWOT analysis not only can provide invaluable information to support the forecasting process but, more importantly, can help identify what type of management you have in place. The responses you receive provide invaluable information as to whether the party completing the SWOT analysis is nothing more than a front-line manager (a captain needing direction) or a bona fide businessperson (the colonel leading the charge).

Next up, we discuss two different forecasting strategies or approaches used by most businesses: *top-down* versus *bottom-up*. *Top-down* forecasting is exactly how it sounds (i.e., the top line for a company, which is sales), as it starts with projecting critical sales revenue data, including sales unit volumes (by all significant product lines or SKUs), pricing by product, any potential sales discounts, seasonality in sales, customer contact to sales timing relationships, and similar data. Once this information is incorporated into the forecast model, the balance of the forecast model, including cost of sales, direct operating expenses, business overhead expenses, and other expenses or income (for the income statement), as well as all critical balance sheet assumptions, are incorporated by utilizing relationships or correlations rather than inputting hard data and information. For example, using a top-down forecasting model, the number of sales representatives required and any commissions earned would be determined based on X number of product sales at Y price. A relationship for the business might be established that states for every 250,000 units of products sold, one senior sales rep is required and would earn a commission of 5% on the sales.

Using a bottom-up approach is quite different as, although certain key correlations or relationships may be incorporated into the forecast model, this approach tends to be much more detailed and includes a large number of hard or firm data points and assumptions being built into the forecast model. For example, in a top-down approach, an expense estimate of $1,000 per month per sales rep may be input to capture all travel, lodging, meals, and entertainment-related costs. In other words, estimated sales revenue drives the number of sales reps, which drives the monthly TLM&E expense. In a bottom-up approach, an estimate of each type of expense is prepared on a line-by-line basis that then rolls up into a subtotal. Further, sales revenue may be driven by how many sales reps are working or employed, so if 10 sales reps are working any given month and, on average, each sales rep should be able to generate $250,000 of sales, total sales for the month would be forecast at $2.5 million.

Quite often, companies use a hybrid of these two approaches, as almost all financial forecast models utilize some type of correlation and relationship assumptions as well as incorporate hard data for various overhead or fixed costs. The bottom-up approach tends to be better suited for well-established, predictable business models that have a large amount of historical data and operational stability. It also tends to be detailed and static but definitely has use/value within the right business framework, such as when detailed or specific management reporting is required for cost analysis of a bill of material or expense control is a high priority (to track all expenses at a line-item level).

The top-down approach tends to be better suited for newer businesses or companies operating in rapidly changing environments where you need to understand important financial results quickly under different or "what-if" operating scenarios (see the next topic). Top-down forecasting approaches are focused on understanding financial correlations and relationships at a macro level to assist the management team in evaluating multiple operating scenarios with potentially vastly different outcomes. To be quite honest, most properly structured top-down forecasting models end up relying on a select few key business drivers or assumptions that really are "make or break" for the company in terms of producing profitable results. Senior-level management members are usually so well versed in understanding their businesses that once as few as a half dozen assumptions and data inputs that drive sales are known, the senior management team members can usually accurately and quickly calculate what the net profit or loss will be. This is why top-down forecasting models are utilized more frequently at the strategic business planning level (i.e., the macro level of big picture), whereas bottom-up forecasting models are utilized actively at the business tactical and implementation level. Under either approach, the goal is to make it easy for team members to participate in the forecasting process and utilize the financial information to assist with improving operating results.

One concept that is strongly associated with the top-down forecasting approach is the *what-if* analysis. It should be obvious that the purpose of the what-if analysis is just like it sounds – that is, what will the results or impact be if this situation or set of events occurs? For example, if a company has to implement a significant product price reduction to match the competition, a what-if analysis will help it quickly calculate and decipher the potential impact on its operating results and associated cash flows. The reason the what-if analysis is easier to use with a top-down forecast approach is that the goal of this analysis tool is to focus on the macro-level impact (to a business) from a potential material change in key business operating metrics. Thus, by being able to change 6 to 12 key variables or forecast assumptions, a management team can quickly assess the impact on the business (which is one of the key strengths of the top-down forecasting approach). This is not to say that what-if analyses cannot be generated using a bottom-up forecasting approach, but when focusing on macro-level company operating results, starting at the top with sales revenue and watching the waterfall impact on overall operations is a particularly useful and powerful analysis for senior management.

We would also like to mention that what-if analyses are extremely helpful when preparing multiple versions of the financial forecasts, which almost all companies do (or should do). It is common practice for companies to produce high, medium, and low versions of the financial forecasts to assist with business planning and evaluate different operating scenarios. Having this information available well in advance will allow a business to build different plans to ensure that financial performance targets are achieved. For example, if sales revenue is trending down, management can develop a plan that identifies expenses to cut and by how much and when. Conversely, if the company is having a strong year, this may dictate that additional capital may be needed to support the unanticipated growth (again, allowing management to identify when, what, and how much will be needed).

As you will see in Exhibits 10.1 through 10.3, the forecast operating results from our high, medium, and low scenarios are vastly different and indicate that management will need to have proactive plans in place to address potential underperformance issues. By the way, another version of the forecast model that companies have incorporated into their planning process is the "Arm" (which stands for Armageddon) version – or when all hell breaks loose. Companies generally keep a tight lid on this version as whether you are dealing with internal or external parties, nobody wants to entice unwarranted panic.

Finally, we close this section by discussing the value and benefits of employing *rolling forecasts* (e.g., 12 months, 18 months, or longer). The purpose of utilizing rolling forecasts is to always have at least (and preferably longer than) one year's visibility on your business's operating performance at any point in time. For example, if a business uses a standard FYE of 12/31/20, a 12-month rolling forecast model updated at, let us say, the third quarter ending 9/30/20 would provide visibility for the 12-month period of 10/1/20 through 9/30/21. After each month, the forecast model is "rolled" forward as part of the company's ongoing planning process to provide executive management with the proper business visibility.

Companies often utilize rolling forecasts to assist with managing their business interests as summarized in the following two examples:

1. *Recast Operating Results:* In our example above, a company could combine the actual operating results for the nine months of operations ending 9/30/20 with the updated three months of forecast operating results for the period of 10/1/20 through 12/31/20 to produce recast operating results for FYE 12/31/20. We use the term *recast* in the context of combining actual operating results with updated forecast operating results to produce revised or recast operating results for a specific time period. Companies often need to provide both internal and external parties with updated outlooks on a periodic basis and will utilize recast operating results to achieve this objective.

2. *Operational Pivots:* Companies that may experience an unexpected shock to their operations (e.g., COVID-19 shutdowns in March of 2020) can utilize rolling forecasts to reset operating targets and objectives for internal management planning purposes. For example, employee commission or bonus plans can be adjusted (based on a revised 12-month outlook) to reflect a new operating norm that was not anticipated. This allows the company to proactively manage difficult environments as well as effectively communicate with the employee base.

Other examples and benefits of utilizing rolling forecasts could be presented but the primary purpose remains the same: to provide forward-looking visibility, over the appropriate time period, that is clear, concise, and complete. This forecasting strategy can prove to be invaluable for companies operating in dynamic, rapidly changing, or unstable business environments, which today is more important than ever before.

FORECAST EXAMPLES

Thus far in this chapter we have covered the topic of forecasts from a conceptual perspective, so now we will offer examples of financial forecasts for our fictious company. Each exhibit will present high, medium, and low case forecasts, with Exhibit 10.1 presenting the income statement, Exhibit 10.2 presenting the balance sheet, and Exhibit 10.3 presenting the statement of cash flows. We call out a couple of key issues in each exhibit to help you understand the importance of preparing multiple forecast versions.

Exhibit 10.1 presents the income statement. Overall, the operating results in the high and medium versions of the forecast model appear reasonable. Solid sales growth, strong profitability, and key financial ratios, including the current ratio (Chapter 8) and the debt service coverage ratio (Chapter 9), are more than adequate. Turning our attention to the low version, significant concerns start to emerge or, in the words of Scooby Doo, "Ruh-roh." On top of the company performing poorly with negative YOY sales growth and basically operating at a breakeven level, two important ratios need further attention.

First, the company's current ratio has fallen below 2.0 (to 1.96). This may appear to still be relatively strong but if the debt facility has a covenant that requires the company to maintain a current ratio above 2.0, then the company may be technically in default. The same goes for the debt service coverage ratio; if the debt facility has a covenant that requires this ratio be 1.5 or above (not at all unreasonable for lenders), then again, the company may be in technical default. Obviously, the company is not in default of these covenants today and does not expect to be in default, as even under the medium case forecast the company has more than enough breathing room. But for management purposes, having a clear understanding of at what operating performance level does the company begin to operate under financial stress is extremely helpful so that if the business does head south, the executive management team can plan for and implement necessary adjustments (e.g., expense reductions) to avoid a rather messy situation with the lender.

EXHIBIT 10.1 Unaudited Income Statement Forecast – High, Medium, and Low

Unaudited - Prepared by Company Management

QW Example Tech., Inc.
Unaudited Financial Statements
Forecasts - H/M/L
For the Fiscal Year Ending
12/31/2021

Income Statement - Forecast for the Fiscal Year Ending	High - FYE 12/31/2021	% of Net Rev.	Medium - FYE 12/31/2021	% of Net Rev.	Low - FYE 12/31/2021	% of Net Rev.
Key Performance Indicators:						
Revenue per Full-Time Employee	$635,667		$559,000		$445,667	
Product Sales, Avg. Order Value (net)	$19,800		$19,800		$12,467	
Software Platform & SAAS Sales:						
SAAS Sales, Total Customer Accounts	700		700		700	
SAAS Sales, Total Earned Avg. per Account	$115,000		$98,571		$82,143	
Macro Level Analysis:						
Year-Over-Year Sales Growth	32.07%		16.14%		-7.41%	
Gross Margin	68.20%		65.69%		63.00%	
Operating Income Margin	19.41%		11.90%		1.95%	
Debt Service Coverage Ratio	8.28		4.87		1.42	
Current Ratio	2.35		2.19		1.96	
Revenue:						
Software Platform & SAAS Sales	$80,500,000	84.43%	$69,000,000	82.29%	$57,500,000	86.01%
Product Sales	$16,500,000	17.30%	$16,500,000	19.68%	$11,000,000	16.45%
Other Sales, Discounts, & Allowances	($1,650,000)	-1.73%	($1,650,000)	-1.97%	($1,650,000)	-2.47%
Net Revenue	$95,350,000	100.00%	$83,850,000	100.00%	$66,850,000	100.00%
Costs of Goods Sold:						
Direct Product Costs	$9,075,000	9.52%	$9,075,000	10.82%	$6,600,000	9.87%
Wages & Burden	$20,247,500	21.23%	$18,690,000	22.29%	$17,132,500	25.63%
Direct Overhead	$750,000	0.79%	$750,000	0.89%	$750,000	1.12%
Other Costs of Goods Sold	$250,000	0.26%	$250,000	0.30%	$250,000	0.37%
Total Costs of Goods Sold	$30,322,500	31.80%	$28,765,000	34.31%	$24,732,500	37.00%
Gross Profit	$65,027,500	68.20%	$55,085,000	65.69%	$42,117,500	63.00%
Gross Margin	68.20%		65.69%		63.00%	
Direct Operating Expenses:						
Advertising, Promotional, & Selling	$8,050,000	8.44%	$7,590,000	9.05%	$6,900,000	10.32%
Personnel Wages, Burden, & Compensation	$6,197,750	6.50%	$6,288,750	7.50%	$5,682,250	8.50%
Facility Operating Expenses	$7,200,000	7.55%	$6,600,000	7.87%	$6,000,000	8.98%
Other Operating Expenses	$619,775	0.65%	$628,875	0.75%	$568,225	0.85%
Total Direct Operating Expenses	$22,067,525	23.14%	$21,107,625	25.17%	$19,150,475	28.65%
Contribution Profit	$42,959,975	45.06%	$33,977,375	40.52%	$22,967,025	34.36%
Contribution Margin	45.06%		40.52%		34.36%	
Corporate Expenses & Overhead:						
Corporate Marketing, Branding, & Promotional	$4,000,000	4.20%	$3,250,000	3.88%	$2,750,000	4.11%
Research, Development, & Design	$14,302,500	15.00%	$14,673,750	17.50%	$13,370,000	20.00%
Corporate Overhead & Support	$3,750,000	3.93%	$3,750,000	4.47%	$3,250,000	4.86%
Depreciation & Amortization Expense	$2,396,905	2.51%	$2,325,833	2.77%	$2,290,298	3.43%
Total Operating Expenses	$24,449,405	25.64%	$23,999,583	28.62%	$21,660,298	32.40%
Operating Income (EBIT)	$18,510,570	19.41%	$9,977,792	11.90%	$1,306,727	1.95%
Operating Margin (EBIT Margin)	19.41%		11.90%		1.95%	
Other Expenses (Income):						
Other Expenses, Income, & Discontinued Ops.	$500,000	0.52%	$500,000	0.60%	$500,000	0.75%
Interest Expense	$525,000	0.55%	$525,000	0.63%	$525,000	0.79%
Total Other Expenses (Income)	$1,025,000	1.07%	$1,025,000	1.22%	$1,025,000	1.53%
Net Income (Loss) Before Taxes	$17,485,570	18.34%	$8,952,792	10.68%	$281,727	0.42%
Income Tax Expense (Benefit)	$6,119,950	6.42%	$3,133,477	3.74%	$98,605	0.15%
Net Income (Loss) After Taxes	$11,365,621	11.92%	$5,819,315	6.94%	$183,123	0.27%

Issues are present w/performance and debt covenants.

Further expense cuts may be needed in these areas.

We now turn our attention to the balance sheet presented in Exhibit 10.2. Here again we provide high, medium, and low forecast scenarios for evaluation and draw your attention to a couple of items. First, you will notice that the ending inventory balance in the low version is actually higher than the high version. This may make sense on the surface, as FYE 2021 product sales

EXHIBIT 10.2   Unaudited Balance Sheet Forecast – High, Medium, and Low

Unaudited - Prepared by Company Management

QW Example Tech., Inc.
Unaudited Financial Statements
Forecasts – H/M/L
For the Fiscal Year Ending
12/31/2021

Balance Sheet – Forecast Period Ending Assets	High - FYE 12/31/2021	Medium - FYE 12/31/2021	Low - FYE 12/31/2021
Current Assets:			
Cash & Equivalents	$22,476,742	$16,366,229	$9,251,370
Accounts Receivable, Net	$11,918,750	$10,481,250	$9,191,875
Inventory, LCM	$1,512,500	$1,701,563	$2,200,000
Prepaid Expenses	$321,913	$283,088	$225,694
Total Current Assets	$36,229,905	$28,832,130	$20,868,938
Long-Term Operating & Other Assets:			
Property, Plant, Equipment, & Machinery	$10,945,000	$10,447,500	$10,198,750
Accumulated Depreciation	($6,249,286)	($6,178,214)	($6,142,679)
Net Property, Plant, & Equipment	$4,695,714	$4,269,286	$4,056,071
Other Assets:			
Intangible Assets & Goodwill, Net	$11,666,667	$11,666,667	$11,666,667
Other Assets	$187,500	$187,500	$187,500
Total Long-Term Operating & Other Assets	$16,549,881	$16,123,452	$15,910,238
Total Assets	**$52,779,786**	**$44,955,582**	**$36,779,177**

(Annotation: Company pivoting away from product sales yet inventory balance remains high. Valuation problem may be present.)

Balance Sheet – Forecast Period Ending Liabilities	High - FYE 12/31/2021	Medium - FYE 12/31/2021	Low - FYE 12/31/2021
Current Liabilities:			
Accounts Payable	$2,979,688	$2,620,313	$2,068,172
Accrued Liabilities & Other	$889,955	$868,050	$788,695
Current Portion of Debt	$2,000,000	$2,000,000	$2,000,000
Income Taxes Payable	$1,529,987	$783,369	$24,651
Other Current Liabilities & Deferred Revenue	$8,050,000	$6,900,000	$5,750,000
Total Current Liabilities	$15,449,630	$13,171,732	$10,631,518
Long-Term Liabilities:			
Notes Payable & Other Long-Term Debt	$4,000,000	$4,000,000	$4,000,000
Other Long-term Liabilities	$700,000	$700,000	$700,000
Total Long-Term Liabilities	$4,700,000	$4,700,000	$4,700,000
Total Liabilities	**$20,149,630**	**$17,871,732**	**$15,331,518**
Stockholders' Equity			
Capital Stock – Common	$10,000,000	$10,000,000	$10,000,000
Capital Stock – Preferred	$8,000,000	$8,000,000	$8,000,000
Dividends	($640,000)	($640,000)	($640,000)
Retained Earnings	$3,904,536	$3,904,536	$3,904,536
Current Earnings (Loss)	$11,365,621	$5,819,315	$183,123
Total Stockholders' Equity	$32,630,156	$27,083,850	$21,447,659
Total Liabilities & Stockholders' Equity	**$52,779,786**	**$44,955,582**	**$36,779,177**

(Annotation: Why is dividend being paid with breakeven operating results? Preferred guaranteed return.)

Confidential - Property of QW Example Tech., Inc.

in the low version are forecast to reach only $11 million versus $16.5 million in the high version (so lower sales equals more inventory on hand and a higher value). However, it may also mean that the company's inventory is rapidly becoming obsolete and it is becoming harder and harder to sell, raising an

EXHIBIT 10.3 Unaudited Statement of Cash Flows Forecast – High, Medium, and Low

Unaudited - Prepared by Company Management

QW Example Tech., Inc.
Unaudited Financial Statements
Forecasts – H/M/L
For the Fiscal Year Ending
12/31/2021

Statement of Cash Flows - Forecast For the Twelve-Month Period Ending	High - FYE 12/31/2021	Medium - FYE 12/31/2021	Low - FYE 12/31/2021
Net Profit (Loss)	$11,365,621	$5,819,315	$183,123
Operating Activities, Cash provided (used):			
Depreciation & Amortization	$2,396,905	$2,325,833	$2,290,298
Decrease (increase) in trade receivables	($2,893,750)	($1,456,250)	($166,875)
Decrease (increase) in inventory	$328,500	$139,438	($359,000)
Decrease (increase) in other current assets	$3,087	$41,912	$99,306
Increase (decrease) in trade payables	$984,688	$625,313	$73,172
Increase (decrease) in accrued liabilities	$39,955	$18,050	($61,305)
Increase (decrease) in other liabilities	$4,463,237	$2,566,619	$657,901
Net Cash Flow from Operating Activities	$16,688,242	$10,080,229	$2,716,620
Investing Activities, Cash provided (used):			
Capital Expenditures	($995,000)	($497,500)	($248,750)
Investments in Other Assets	($62,500)	($62,500)	($62,500)
Net Cash Flow from Investing Activities	($1,057,500)	($560,000)	($311,250)
Financing Activities, Cash provided (used):			
Dividends or Distributions Paid	($640,000)	($640,000)	($640,000)
Sale (repurchase) of Equity	$0	$0	$0
Proceeds from Issuance of Debt	$0	$0	$0
Repayments of Debt	($2,000,000)	($2,000,000)	($2,000,000)
Other Financing Activities	$75,000	$75,000	$75,000
Net Cash Flow from Financing Activities	($2,565,000)	($2,565,000)	($2,565,000)
Other Cash Flow Adjustments – Asset Impairment	$0	$0	$0
Net Increase (decrease) in Cash & Equivalents	$13,065,742	$6,955,229	($159,630)
Beginning Cash & Equivalents Balance	$9,411,000	$9,411,000	$9,411,000
Ending Cash & Equivalents Balance	$22,476,742	$16,366,229	$9,251,370

Confidential - Property of QW Example Tech., Inc.

> Breakeven year yet produces $2.7 million in net cash flow. However, almost all committed to guaranteed debt and dividend payments.

all-important question as to whether the inventory is actually worth $2.2 million or should management write off a portion of the inventory as worthless (which means the company would have to incur an additional expense and most likely push it from profitability under the low version to a loss – Ouch!).

Second, you may ask why the company would pay a dividend when at best it is operating at a breakeven level. This is an excellent question indeed and one that we explore more in Chapter 17 on understanding the cap table. Basically, what it comes down to is that when the company raises preferred equity, this tranche of equity comes with a guaranteed annual dividend of 8%, regardless of the profit level. Hence, the company is required to pay the dividend and if it does not, it would be in default of the capital raise agreement.

Finally, we reach the statement of cash flows as presented in Exhibit 10.3, which also sheds additional valuable information in the low version of the forecast model. Reviewing the statement of cash flows in more detail, you will notice that the low version of the forecast model produces approximately $2.7 million of positive cash flow from operations, which is basically 100% consumed by the set or guaranteed financing related payments (for the company) of roughly $2.6 million, which is comprised of preferred equity dividend payments and debt repayments. Okay, so the good news is that the company can generate enough internal positive cash flow to cover the guaranteed payments, but looking closer, this really could become a problem as in effect the company is using short-term working capital to repay long-term financial commitments (an imbalance that should be avoided).

We could highlight additional issues and findings with the financial information presented in the forecast versions but the points we would like to emphasize here are as follows. First, having complete financial forecasts, including the income statement, balance sheet, and statement of cash flows, is critical for management planning purposes. Second, the power and importance of utilizing the what-if forecasting tool is on full display. And third, even in a forecast, the all-important concept that accounting (and finance) is more of an art than a science holds true.

FORECAST SECRETS AND THE BIG PICTURE

Chapter 1 of this book introduced you to the big-three financial statements and the purpose and importance of each one. It was a relatively long chapter, as is this chapter on financial forecasting, as both cover a large amount of material. Our goal is not to bury you with too much information (i.e., burying you in the BS) but rather to help you understand just how important CART financial information really is and how top management teams utilize the accounting and finance departments as a competitive weapon. With this said, we would like to summarize this chapter by rehashing some invaluable gems and secrets related to financial forecasting:

- Graduate: Bottom-up forecast models are valuable tools for businesses but for you to move up in the executive management hierarchy, you will need to graduate and become comfortable using top-down forecasts. Top executives usually have such a solid understanding of the economic structure of their business that they can simply change a select number of critical operating assumptions and will almost immediate know what the end result will be (e.g., a change to top-line sales revenue will lead to a bottom-line result). To be an effective executive-level manager, you need to efficiently understand the macro-level impact on your business from changing economic conditions. That is, you "can't see the forest for the trees."

➤ The P&L focus: There is no question that too many businesses focus first and only on the P&L when preparing forecasts. It should be clear from this chapter just how important the balance sheet and cash flow statement are, especially as they relate to cash flow and third-party capital source management.

➤ External/internal: Internal financial forecasts include significant amounts of detail and confidential information that should not be distributed to external parties. Not only is the level of detail on a line-item basis excessive but the high and low versions of the forecast model should not be distributed externally (as these are for internal management use). Again, what a business distributes to external parties is vastly different than for internal consumption.

- Tone it down: Most companies produce forecasts that derive financial data from multiple internal operating divisions (e.g., a company may have a dozen operating divisions which they consolidate to prepare a company-wide forecast). What tends to happen during the con-solidation process is that everyone is a bit too optimistic so when the combined results are produced, the operat-ing results look great (see the high version in Exhib-its 10.1 through 10.3). In reality, somewhere along the line certain divisions are going to stumble and not per-form as well, so while it is fine to set internal expecta-tions relatively high, finalizing a company-wide forecast should be toned down to be more realistic (for distribu-tion to external parties, the company's board of direc-tors, etc.). There is nothing worse than overpromising and underdelivering and then having to explain yourself.

CHAPTER 11

Flash Reports and Key Performance Indicators

I FEEL THE NEED FOR SPEED

"I feel the need for speed" was a quote made famous by the character Maverick, played by Tom Cruise, in the movie *Top Gun*. Today, this quote no doubt rings close to home for business executives and senior management across the board as given the digital transformation of the global economy, speed in financial information reporting is no longer an option but a necessity. In today's hyperconnected world that analyzes millions of pieces of data in a split second, the ability to decipher key operating data quickly and efficiently (at a senior management level) is critical.

But speed should not be confused with ultra-short time periods, as not all flash reports are "speed"-centric. Flash reports may be just as effective when produced monthly as opposed to hourly. Effective flash reports provide the right financial information at the right time and in the right format for management to assess critically sensitive operating data.

We should note that this chapter will not be overly long as we have already referenced the concept of flash reports and key performance indicators (KPIs) throughout this book and in numerous contexts (e.g., using in forecasts, reported in financial statements, etc.). However, we felt it would be helpful to provide some additional examples of flash reports and KPIs that are used in today's ecommerce or direct-to-consumer (DTC) industries given the rise of online shopping at the expense of traditional brick-and-mortar retail stores.

PRIMARY FLASH REPORT CHARACTERISTICS

Flash reports represent nothing more than a timely snapshot of critical company operating and financial data, which is then used to support the ongoing operations of the business. All types of flash reports are used in business, ranging from a printed circuit board manufacturing company evaluating its book-to-bill ratio on a weekly basis to Walmart reporting hourly sales by selling department by SKU during the holiday season to an auto manufacturer evaluating weekly finished goods inventory levels.

The goal with all flash reports remains the same in that critical business information is delivered to management for review much more frequently. As such, flash reports tend to have the following key attributes present:

> *Simplicity of Report:* Flash reports are generally more simplistic than traditional financial statements and reports. As we discussed in Chapters 1 through 3, the amount of information presented in financial statements and financial reports can be extensive (as the goal is to report on the entire operations of a company). Flash reports are much more focused and designed to capture three to five key operating data points or KPIs that represent critical information to the target audience.

> *Frequency of Report:* Flash reports tend to be produced much more frequently. Unlike the production of financial statements (which generally occurs monthly), flash reports are often produced weekly and, in numerous cases, daily or even hourly. In today's competitive marketplace, management is demanding that information be provided more frequently than ever to stay on top of rapidly changing markets.

> *Critical Data:* Flash reports are designed to capture critical operating and financial performance data of your business or the real information that can make or break your business. As a result, sales activities and/ or volumes are almost always a part of a business's flash reporting effort. Once management has a good handle on the top line, the bottom line should be relatively easy to calculate.

> *Range of Data:* Flash reports are not limited to presenting financial data. Flash reports can be designed to capture all kinds of data,

including retail store foot volume (or customer traffic levels), labor utilization rates, and the like. While the president of a division may want to know how sales are tracking this month, the manufacturing manager will want to keep a close eye on labor hours incurred in the production process.

➤ *Source of Data:* Financial flash reports should obtain their base information from the same accounting and financial information system that produces periodic financial statements, forecasts, and other reports. While the presentation of the information may be different, the source of the information should come from the same transactional basis (of your company).

➤ *Internal Focus:* Flash reports are almost exclusively used for internal management needs and are rarely delivered to external parties. Flash reports are usually more detailed in nature and tend to contain far more confidential data than, say, audited financial statements, and are almost never audited.

➤ *Close Friends with Forecasts:* Flash reports are closely related to the forecasting process. For example, if a company is experiencing a short-term cash flow squeeze, management will need to have access to a rolling 13-week cash flow projection to properly evaluate cash inflows and outflows on a weekly basis. Each week, the rolling 13-week cash flow projection is provided to management for review in the form of a flash report, which is always being updated to look out 13 weeks.

 A critical concept to understand with flash reports is that these reports should act more as a confirmation of your company's performance than a report that offers original information. By this we mean that once the key data in a flash report is evaluated and understood, the resulting impact on other financial and operating results should be relatively straightforward.

For example, if a flash report that presents sales volumes for the first two weeks of February compared to the similar two-week period for the prior year is reporting new sales information, the format of the report and the presentation of the information in the report should be consistent. Thus, management should be able to quickly decipher the results and determine whether the company is performing within expectations and what to expect on the bottom line for the entire month.

KEY PERFORMANCE INDICATORS

If it is not evident yet, it will be after you read this section: Flash reports and KPIs are almost always the absolute best and closest of friends. Flash reports are most beneficial when they effectively combine and report key financial information alongside pivotal KPIs (e.g., a crucial ratio or relationship). For example, when a sales flash report is prepared, it should not only include gross sales dollars but also report net sales dollars (taking into account any discounts), total unit sales, average unit selling price, average order value, and the like. Taking this flash report one step further, it may also report gross profit dollars, gross margin, and other critical information related to how much advertising expense was incurred to generate the sales.

Exhibit 11.1 provides an example of a typical flash report prepared for a business operating in the online retail space (i.e., DTC) that includes KPIs related to the cost of acquiring the customer.

Exhibit 11.1 presents a detail of daily sales data by primary time slot but could just as easily present sales by hour or expand the report to compare daily sales for a week (or longer). The length of time covered in a flash report and the level of detail is determined by the needs of the management team. A couple of items of particular interest in the flash report are the following:

➤ The average order value is highest during the late morning and evening time periods, indicating that the typical customer is purchasing multiple items (most likely for multiple gifts) with each order. During other periods, the average order value is basically the same as the average net unit value (or buying one item per order). This may indicate that the company may want to push more aggressive multiple purchase promotions during the peak buying periods (to drive higher revenue).

➤ Cost per acquisition (CPA) is a critical KPI for companies operating in the DTC space. This calculation compares total direct advertising spends (e.g., on large social media sites such as Instagram and Google) against the net sales revenue to calculate a percentage that the company will most likely attempt to manage within a reasonable range (i.e., from 30% to 45%). An interesting data point is that the CPA for the highest sales period was only 28.75% compared to higher levels for other periods. However, this period also saw the most aggressive sales price discounting at 20%. This may mean that the company left some earnings on the table by discounting too aggressively and is something management should analyze to improve performances moving forward.

EXHIBIT 11.1 DTC Business Unaudited Sales Flash Report

Unaudited - Prepared by Company Management

XYZ DtoC Example, Inc.
Unaudited Sales Flash Report
For SKUs 100–500
Daily for
12/10/2020

Day of Week	Number of Sales	Number of Units Sold	Gross Sales	Average Discount	Net Sales	Avg. Net Order Value	Avg. Net Unit Value	Avg. Gross Margin	Total Gross Profit	Total Adv. Spends	CPA Ratio	Discount + CPA Ratio
Early Morning (midnight until 7:00 a.m.)	32	32	$4,160	10.00%	$3,744	$117	$117	66.00%	$2,471	$1,250	33.39%	43.39%
Late Morning (7:00 a.m. until noon)	104	125	$18,750	15.00%	$15,938	$153	$128	65.00%	$10,359	$5,780	36.27%	51.27%
Early Afternoon (noon until 3:00 p.m.)	56	56	$7,840	5.00%	$7,448	$133	$133	66.00%	$4,916	$3,100	41.62%	46.62%
Late Afternoon and Evening (3:00 p.m. until 7:00 p.m.)	210	263	$32,612	20.00%	$26,090	$124	$99	60.00%	$15,654	$7,500	28.75%	48.75%
Night (7:00 p.m. until midnight)	75	83	$9,545	10.00%	$8,591	$115	$104	67.00%	$5,756	$2,450	28.52%	38.52%
Total	477	558	$72,907	15.22%	$61,810	$130	$111	63.35%	$39,155	$20,080	32.49%	47.71%

Confidential - Property of XYZ DtoC Example, Inc.

Evening shopping period is the best during the holidays as consumers shop most after work. Low CPA ratio is offset by more aggressive discounting. Company may want to evaluate if 20% discounting rate was necessary as more shoppers are active.

The lowest total cost of acquiring the customer was during the night period when advertising rates are lower. The company may want to increase marketing efforts during the night when the costs are lower and shoppers are active.

The level of that which can be completed on these types of flash reports is extensive and often drills down much further to a point that can reconcile a specific time period sales performance with a unique or detailed promotional or advertising campaign that was utilized (e.g., that may use different content). This is a benefit and curse of the modern digital age we live in, as the speed at which a business can access data and operating results is both wonderful but also highly stressful.

Taking our flash report example one step further, we now direct your attention to Exhibit 11.2.

What we have done with this flash report is to prepare an estimated quick or mini-P&L for the month based on our daily sales flash report presented in Exhibit 11.1 and also provided a simple variance analysis against the original forecast for the month. For simplicity, we have assumed that the daily sales and expense information realized on 12/10/20 (refer to Exhibit 11.1) are relatively consistent with the previous days' activity of 12/1/10 through 12/9/20 and are expected to remain at these levels through approximately 12/22/20 (the last big sales day before Christmas) and then fall off dramatically, as sales tend to, post Christmas. Also, the company's operating expenses and SG&A are fixed at $225,000 per month (so no surprises are expected during the month).

Here again, we dive into the operating results and highlight a couple of items:

➤ Net sales revenue is forecast to underperform during the month by approximately $116,000 or 7.6% – definitely not a friendly trend but one that needs to be taken in context with the next observation.

➤ The company's direct advertising and selling expenses are averaging 28%, well below the forecast level of 33%, resulting in a positive variance of $114,000. Hence, even though net sales are below forecast, expenses are trending even lower, allowing the company to potentially overperform for the month (at least based on this mid-month estimate). What the company has figured out is how to sell "smarter" and more efficiently to the customer.

You might notice that we are touching on the concept of completeness again as if a party were only focused on the negative top-line sales trend and did not understand the importance of selling smarter, they might draw an incorrect conclusion on the outlook for the business during the month of December.

EXHIBIT 11.2   DTC Business Audited Mini-P&L Flash Report

Unaudited - Prepared by Company Management

XYZ DtoC Example, Inc.
Unaudited Quick/Mini P&L
For All Product Sales
Estimated for the Month Ending
12/31/2020

Summary Income Statement	Estimated Amount $	% of Rev.	Forecast Amount $	% of Rev.	Variance
Gross Sales Revenue	$1,669,570	100%	$1,750,000	100%	($80,430)
Less: Discounts	($254,130)	-15%	($218,750)	-13%	($35,380)
Net Sales Revenue	$1,415,440	85%	$1,531,250	88%	$115,810)
COGS	$518,779	31%	$535,938	31%	$17,158
Gross Profit	$896,661	54%	$995,313	57%	($98,652)
Direct Advertising & Selling Expenses	$459,832	28%	$574,219	33%	$114,387
Contribution Profit	$436,829	26%	$421,094	24%	$15,735
Average Monthly Company Op. Ex. & SG&A	$225,000	13%	$225,000	13%	$0
Estimated Operating Profit (loss) for Month	$211,829	13%	$196,094	11%	$15,735

Confidential - Property of XYZ DtoC Example, Inc.

Interesting month taking hold in December (peak holiday sales). Weaker sales offset by significantly lower advertising & selling expense so company tracking ahead of schedule.

Closing out this section of the chapter, we would like to remind our readers to keep these two thoughts in mind: First, flash reports are not solely reserved for just financial data or dollar amounts, as invaluable information needs to be reported and understood that involves qualitative data. In the DTC world, KPIs and critical data points include advertising rates for number of impressions, clickthrough rates for advertisements, and cart fill and abandonment rates, as well as conversion rates. We do not explain each of these items, as the goal is to emphasize the importance of generating qualitatively based flash reports.

Second, our flash report examples have been isolated to a specific industry that is sensitive to this type of reporting. We chose this industry given the rapid shift in consumer buying habits (from brick-and-mortar retail to DTC) as well as being a great example of flash reporting and critical KPIs. But please note that all industries ranging from auto manufacturing to public utilities to banking to you name it will aggressively implement the use of flash reporting to improve the overall effectiveness of management's performance. The key is to design, implement, and analyze flash reports and KPIs that offer the most value to the business.

A FEW PARTING THOUGHTS

The economic reality for most businesses is quite simple. That is, a business or operating unit's financial performance generally comes down to three to four key performance metrics or economic drivers that are "make or break" in terms of realizing positive or negative results. These include understanding top-line sales (volume and net price), direct costs of goods sold (know your gross margin), and operating expenses (keep in check). Master your knowledge of this financial information and you should be able to predict your income statement results in advance, as once you know your sales figures, you should have a clear/reliable understanding of profits.

But, as stressed throughout this book with the concept of completeness, it is one thing to be able to efficiently understand the income statement from a top-down perspective but something else to understand the impact on the company's entire financial picture. That is, I know my sales, gross margin, and operating expenses and I am confident with the net profit or loss that will be generated. Okay, this is great, but what if the conversation moves one step further to understand the impact on cash resources and liquidity?

And this is what really separates the financial adults (experts) from the children (novices). Being able to translate the results of the income statement to their corresponding influence on the balance sheet and statement of cash flows, to know in advance and with confidence what type of impact may transpire on a company's cash resources, liquidity, and capital needs, is essential in gaining the trust of the executive management team, board of directors, and external capital sources.

CHAPTER 12

Wall Street's Latest Trick – Financial Engineering

WHAT FINANCIAL ENGINEERING IS NOT

We start this chapter on financial engineering by addressing the question of why we have elected to include this subject matter in the "how" portion of the book. The answer is simple and comes down to one key concept: Financial engineering, whether utilized by Wall Street or Main Street (i.e., private businesses), offers a lesson on how businesses can massage, tweak, adjust, and, for lack of a better term, manipulate financial information and results to present a financial story that helps achieve a specific goal or objective (which usually involves increasing a company's valuation).

Before we dive into the concept of financial engineering and what it entails, it is helpful to identify what financial engineering is *not*. We want to put out of your mind any preconceived notions about the topics of fraudulent financial reporting or heavy-handed manipulation of accounting and other deliberately misleading information put into financial reports.

There are two specific points that are important to understand:

1. Financial engineering does not refer to the intentional misreporting and misleading presentation of accounting transactions and financial operating results. It does not refer to cooking the books. While we

143

would love to recall some of the great accounting frauds of the past (e.g., Enron), this subject would warrant a whole book to itself. We just point out here that almost all "great" accounting frauds were supported by executive-level management collusion. Multiple members of the executive management team worked in complicity to report financial information with the willful intent to deceive and mislead. We offer here only a couple of advisory points to remember when it comes to fraudulent financial information. Be on the lookout for any signs of executive-level collusion, such as boards of directors that are not truly independent. Be careful if the CPA auditor of the financial report is relatively unknown. Finally, be extra careful of tightly controlled insider-operated businesses, which are more conducive to accounting and financial reporting abuse.

2. Financial engineering usually does not refer to companies adopting aggressive accounting methods and highly favorable estimates for recording transactions and reporting financial operating results. Using aggressive accounting methods by itself does not represent a fraudulent activity as long as the accounting methods fall within the guidelines of generally accepted accounting principles (GAAP). The use of one accounting method over another is a decision best left for the company's management team, board of directors, and independent auditors to resolve and agree upon. With this said, we would offer a tip as it relates to sniffing out companies that may be utilizing more aggressive accounting methods than are justified: aggressive accounting methods can be used to accelerate sales revenue and defer expenses, thereby inflating earnings. While this makes the income statement look good and gives the appearance of strong profits, do not forget that the income statement is generally the easiest of the three fundamental financial statements to manipulate. This is one reason we emphasize the importance of understanding how cash is generated and consumed in a business, which can readily be found in the cash flows statement.

WHAT FINANCIAL ENGINEERING IS

So now that we know what financial engineering is not, let us explore what financial engineering refers to. First, we encounter a problem. The term has more than one meaning. Broadly speaking, it refers to the use of highly sophisticated mathematical methods and computer-based algorithms for analyzing financial reports data. Here we use the term *financial engineering* in an important but much more limited sense.

In the rest of the chapter, we use the term to refer to going a step beyond simple ratios to use other techniques for analyzing and reconfiguring financial report information. This additional layer of analysis may very well sway or shift the reader's sentiment about a company's operating performance and financial position. The primary goal of financial engineering, as we use the term in this chapter, is to assist external parties with gaining a better understanding of a business's reported operating results and financial position. One example of how businesses utilize financial engineering strategies directly in their financial reports concerns the issue of *extraordinary gains and losses*.

Companies have been able to produce financial statements that present core operating results and carve out extreme or unique, one-time events that negatively impacted net profits (called extraordinary events) during a specific reporting period. For example, a manufacturing company based in the South might have experienced a massive, once-in-a-generation loss from a devastating weather event such as a hurricane. With the loss being so significant and the event so unusual, it would not be expected to recur for quite a while, so it could be captured as a one-time loss reported as *other expenses* in the income statement (below the operating income level). By carving out this rather unusual expense, an external reader of the financial statements could clearly and efficiently understand why the company incurred such a large loss, allowing him or her to focus on the remaining base operations to evaluate the company's financial performance.

Up to this point, we agree that presenting more complete, accurate, and revealing financial operating results in the financial statements is warranted and beneficial to outside parties. But it is also at this point where the concept of modern-day financial engineering needs to be appreciated and that accounting as an "art" form versus a science needs to be clearly understood by defining financial engineering in the simplest form.

Financial engineering is based in the idea of taking GAAP financial statements and accounting information (as presented) and then engineering, or rearranging the information into a different format, structure, comparison, and so on. The *engineered* data should offer invaluable additional information and perspectives for the purpose of allowing users to make better-informed business decisions. Without the engineered information, external parties may depend solely on a financial report, which can manipulate or distort information that could lead external parties to different conclusions on a company's financial performance and position.

When undertaking financial engineering, you take GAAP financial information and reconfigure it into a different financial framework. In doing this you will start to notice a series of rather commonly used terms and expressions frequently associated with companies that present financially engineered information. These terms, usually abbreviated with acronyms, include non-GAAP, adjusted GAAP, EBITDA, or adjusted EBITDA, proforma results, sales bookings, and free cash flow. The list goes on and on. Your antennae should definitely be raised, and you should plan to apply additional scrutiny to the information when this type of terminology appears. The risk of the information not being in compliance with GAAP increases because consistency and comparability may be lacking when it comes to how companies define, interpret, and present this information. Furthermore, companies may be much more selective in the type of information they present (to influence/direct a reader toward a specific conclusion). *In short, financially engineered information, by itself, is not fraudulent in nature but rather a somewhat subjective method of reporting financial results that warrants additional scrutiny from external parties.*

Ultimately, it is up to the financial report reader to decide how important the financially engineered information is, how credible it is, and whether it should be relied upon. There is no real school for this other than knowledge and experience, which we hope to help you build, at least a little bit, with our book and specifically this chapter.

Common types of financial engineering

Now that we have helped provide a little more clarity on what constitutes financial engineering, it is time to consider a handful of financial engineering examples that have been used (or) abused, over the past two or more decades. This list is by no means all-inclusive but rather is designed to provide a smattering of the breadth of tools and strategies used by companies to highlight (and we use this term with an abundance of caution) certain operating results.

To start, we offer three examples of financial engineering that are fully blessed by GAAP but need deeper dives to properly understand a company's financial performance:

1. **Discontinued Operations and/or Extraordinary Events:** We previously touched on this topic as it relates to properly disclosing an

extraordinary, one-time event that is material and unusual in nature. We agree with this concept, as these types of events are best reported in a clear, concise, and separate manner. Where companies begin to push the limit on this concept and enter into somewhat of a gray zone can be found in two primary areas.

a. First, are we truly dealing with a one-off event or does the company have a habit of reporting these types of losses year after year? You would be amazed at how many companies convince themselves that a bad business decision warrants a separate disclosure in the financial statements as an extraordinary event (assuming that the loss was beyond the control of management). When a pattern of continued losses from these types of events emerges period after period, you must ask if it is really a one-off event or just a means to deflect external parties from bad business decisions being made by the company's management team.

b. Second, the definition of what constitutes an extraordinary event is often very subjective. GAAP and other accounting pronouncements attempt to provide guidance on this subject but, ultimately, the disclosure decision is generally made by the company's executive management team and external auditors. Furthermore, definitions may change over time when operating in different business environments, when new management teams are brought on board, and so on. This leads to consistency concerns over different reporting periods, which makes it difficult to compare performance over time.

2. **Stock Buybacks:** Stock buybacks have been around for decades, but have really kicked in since 2012 as a result of ultra-cheap debt being available and from the benefits received from the 2017 Tax Cuts and Jobs Act, making stock buybacks one of the hottest topics in the financial community. When a company buys back its own stock the results often look great on the surface. This is because when EPS is calculated as profit and divided over fewer outstanding shares, it increases. From a GAAP perspective, this is technically correct because the remaining shareholders have the right to increased earnings moving forward (so EPS would be higher). But digging deeper, you must ask if this type of transaction or event represents real internal growth that is sustainable year over year or whether it has actually weakened the company's financial position by increasing debt levels (thus increasing financial leverage) or reducing cash holdings (and liquidity).

3. **Tax Rates and Jurisdictions:** In 2017, the Trump Administration spearheaded a meaningful change to the tax code, which included, among other things, a significant decrease to corporate marginal tax rates. Of course, this was hailed by the corporate world as a significant win. By lowering income tax rates, corporate profits would automatically increase, which was generally the case. But again, and similar to the concept of stock buybacks, the question of sustainability needs to be addressed, as when external parties compared a company's 2017 net profit (assuming a 35% tax rate) against its 2018 net profit (assuming a 21% tax rate), the resulting appearance of significant growth in EPS was artificially bumped higher for a one-year period (e.g., whether the company really realized a 22% increase in earnings). However, when 2018 and 2019 operating results are compared, the impact of the lower tax rate will have passed, and a more stable picture of real earnings growth emerges. This concept can also be expanded to companies utilizing or leveraging low-tax-rate jurisdictions to massage net income (e.g., sheltering earnings in foreign countries that have exceptionally low corporate tax rates). Again, the question must be asked whether this is a real benefit or simply a company being more interested in playing a shell game with taxable income. The lesson here is simple: It is important to not rely on changing tax laws or profit-shifting strategies (to manage earnings so they appear higher) as a cure-all for what ails a business. (In the end, if a company is losing money, income taxes are really a moot point.) It goes without saying that proper comparisons at equivalent tax rates should be completed.

Next, we provide three examples of what we will call the *real* or *pure* financial engineering strategies that are outside the scope of GAAP but are frequently utilized by companies:

1. **EBITDA and Addbacks:** First we need to ask the question as to why EBITDA is important. Simply put, EBITDA is a measurement of internal cash flow (a) used to evaluate a company's ability to service debt or support distributions/dividends and (b) relied upon as a basis for valuing a business (e.g., when one company is looking to buy another business). It should make sense that a higher EBITDA generally translates into the ability for a company to support higher debt levels. It also indicates that the company's value is higher.

   Special Note: We need to emphasize that the concept of EBITDA is subjective and for the most part beyond the scope of GAAP (so it needs to be taken with a grain of salt). But where the real fun begins with EBITDA is when companies start to discuss or disclose *adjusted* EBITDA with operating performance addbacks. "What are add-backs?" you might ask. Addbacks as such are really nothing more than management's assessment of either increased revenue (that should have been earned but for some reason was not) or decreased expenses (that will be nonrecurring) that should be included or added back in calculating adjusted EBITDA to support a valuation analysis, debt service calculation, and so on. At this point, it should be abundantly clear just how badly not only EBITDA, but addbacks can be abused to inflate earnings and company valuations to achieve a financial objective. Countless examples of the aggressive use of addbacks to inflate EBITDA could be provided, but the general concept we are driving home is that adjusting EBITDA is a very common strategy and a negotiating point when negotiating a financial transaction that can be manipulated beyond belief.

2. **Sales Revenue Recognition:** One of the hottest and most important topics in GAAP relates to recognizing sales and determining when the earnings process is complete. More than a few accountants and authoritative groups have weighed in on this subject as with so many types of sales transactions utilized in the global economy today there is no shortage of opinions and fact patterns available to help guide a company with recognizing sales revenue. Furthermore, there are several subjective elements that must be taken into consideration when recognizing sales revenue, ranging from the validity of the sale to begin with (at the initial point of sales) through to the ultimate collectability of the sale (can the customer even pay). What companies have begun to do on a more frequent basis is to present a non-GAAP sales revenue to reflect, for example, just how many bookings they have (but have not yet delivered to the market or have not satisfied the tests to fully realize the sales revenue in the current period). Is this useful information? Absolutely. But does it mean the company has earned the revenue/sales? Absolutely not! So, take care to understand the difference between GAAP-recognized sales revenue and the countless other forms of non-GAAP sales revenue a company may disclose.

3. **Proforma Operating Results:** Another quite common non-GAAP financial disclosure and analysis companies like to provide relates to presenting *proforma* operating results. For example, a company may

undertake a major acquisition toward the end of the year. Suppose the acquisition holds the promise of significant expense reductions being realized over the next two to three years with the combined operations because economies of scale are realized with large personnel expense reductions anticipated. So, a company may take actual, audited GAAP-based financial results for both companies and then present a hypothetical combination of the two entities as if they were operating together and just how many costs/expenses could be eliminated. Again, this information may be interesting, but is it 100% factual and supported by an audit? Generally no, and it may not be in 100% compliance with GAAP. One thing is for certain: The information is highly dependent on management assessments and estimates that are based on forward-looking statements that may or may not come to fruition.

Final word

We conclude our discussion on financial engineering by emphasizing once again that there is nothing inherently illegal or dishonest about providing supplemental information, which is often especially useful to external parties. But in the same breath, it is important to note that this type of information tends to be much more subjective in nature and is provided to sway or influence external-party analysis of a company, often not in conformity with GAAP and generally not audited by an external CPA firm. Red flags should be raised when you see terms like *EBITDA, adjusted GAAP, proforma, non-GAAP, booked revenue* (not yet earned), and the list goes on and on. Make sure you pay close attention to the information and understand the source and purpose of why it is being presented.

PART THREE

WHY FINANCIAL INFORMATION IS SO CRITICAL AND HOW TO USE IT TO YOUR ADVANTAGE

CHAPTER 13

Capitalizing a Business

THE NEED FOR FINANCIAL CAPITAL AND A BUSINESS PLAN

In the final five chapters of the book, we turn our attention from the "What, When, and Where" of preparing financial information (covered in Chapters 1 through 7) and the "How" financial information is analyzed (covered in Chapters 8 through 12) to a final discussion on the "Why" of financial information. I mean, really, why go through all this trouble to prepare complete, accurate, reliable, and timely (CART) financial information and then analyze the financial reports, statements, flash reports, and so on if there is no pot of gold at the end of the rainbow?

While the answer should be obvious (i.e., to build an economically viable business that creates real value), we spend the final five chapters of this book spelling it out in a clear and concise manner covering five main topics:

1. The business plan, types of capital, and a closer look at debt capital (Chapter 13)
2. Improving profits, what is real, and what is imaginary (Chapter 14)
3. How and why businesses are valued (Chapter 15)
4. Business acquisition basics (Chapter 16)
5. The business capitalization table and who owns and controls what (Chapter 17)

The remainder of this chapter provides an overview of options and strategies available to capitalize newly formed businesses as well as how existing businesses evaluate, deploy, and utilize capital with a focus on debt-based capital sources.

THE BUSINESS PLAN

It should go without saying that when either new businesses are formed and launched or an existing business implements a specific strategy (e.g., to drive sales growth, improve earnings per share, restructure current operations, etc.), a well-developed, supported, presented, and communicated business plan is an absolute necessity. Business plans provide a roadmap for company management to implement and execute, as they not only outline the resources that will be required but, more importantly, establish a benchmark on which the company's management team can be evaluated. Further, business plans come in all shapes, sizes, and forms, ranging from an entire company-wide plan (e.g., laying out how a company like General Motors will transition from making cars with combustible engines to producing electronically powered vehicles over X years) to something as simple as establishing a revenue goal for a group of sales reps who service a specific geographical region.

Business plans generally include a wide range of information, data, reports, articles, analyses, assessments, and the list goes on and on. The level of detail included in a business plan is usually dependent on the target audience as what might be presented to an external group of venture capitalists or private equity investors (i.e., much more condensed with limitations on disclosing confidential information) would be significantly different than presenting a business plan to a company's board of directors. Also, you may frequently hear the term "The Deck" referenced, which is nothing more than a condensed version of a business plan presented in an easy to understand, logical, and appealing format (such as a PowerPoint or PDF file).

A macro-level business plan should cover all relevant and critical material, which can basically be broken down into the following five primary buckets:

1. Summarize the market environment. Consider questions such as: What is the current market opportunity or need? What market or industry characteristics and trends are present? What is the size of the market? What competition is present? On the surface, providing

market information should be a no-brainer, yet in practice this is one topic that business plans tend to be weak in addressing, as acquiring reliable and credible third-party market information is much easier said than done.

2. Overview what resources will be required: What physical assets will be needed and when? Will new technology need to be developed? What will the organizational chart (org chart) look like? When will personnel need to be hired? What supply chain considerations are present? Again, the potential list of topics is endless, but it should be focused on key operational functions that are critical to the success of the plan.

3. List the management team: This is relatively simple and straightforward as there is no way a business plan is going to be executed without a strong, experienced, and committed management team being in place.

4. Forecast the potential financial return: Generally speaking, the financial opportunity or return is highlighted with a forecast or proforma income statement that presents multiple years of business operating results (with three to five years of forecast income statements being common).

5. Summarize the amount and type of required financial capital: A conclusion should be drawn not just as to the amount of capital investment a company needs to make to execute the business plan but more importantly, what type of capital (debt or equity) will be needed and, even more critical, what will the capital structure be. The financial capital conclusion is often supported by what is referred to as "sources and uses of funds," which outlines total sources of capital and how the capital will be used or deployed.

 Condensing this even further, here is what a business plan really is – it answers the questions: What is the opportunity, what resources will be needed, who is the management team, what is the potential financial return, and how much capital is needed?

The remainder of this chapter is focused on our fifth point, related to how much and what type of financial capital is needed, as expanding on the first three points above would constitute a book in itself (and financial forecasts and projections were already covered in Chapter 10). But before we move on with our discussion on exploring financial capital in more depth, we would like to remind everyone just how wide the range and scope of business plans can be by providing three very real examples in today's economy:

1. Technology start-ups launched by aspiring entrepreneurs are very much in vogue these days. Silicon Valley represents a hub of the technology world and is constantly evaluating and, when appropriate, investing in the next Tesla or Airbnb (hopefully). New start-ups require significant financial capital to launch, with "equity raises" being the most common form of capital.

2. Large, mature businesses operating in industries ranging from finance/banking to technology powerhouses such as Apple have, over the past 5+ years, undertaken strategies to raise capital through issuing "debt," which in turn is used (along with internal cash resources) to buy back their own stock. We covered this Wall Street tactic in Chapter 12, but it should be remembered that implementing this type of strategy represents just as much of a business plan as a new start-up raising equity capital.

3. To provide another example of a business plan, please think about Exxon for a moment. Here is a company that has operated in the oil and gas industry for over 100 years and has had to weather a serious economic correction in this space (most recently with a collapse in the price of oil, starting in 2014) as well as the current threat and opportunity posed by renewable energy sources. You can imagine the business planning that must be undertaken when evaluating the value of billions of dollars of investments in energy properties and what type of capital the company will require to reposition its business in the renewable space.

The point is that business plans and the conclusion on how much financial capital will be needed are vast, complex, and constantly changing and evolving as market conditions change.

TYPES OF AVAILABLE CAPITAL

With our discussion of business plans out of the way, we can now turn to the options and strategies available to capitalize a business. To keep this simple, capitalizing a business comes down to one of two types – utilizing debt or equity.

We should note that yes, a business can deploy or recycle internal capital that is available from company-generated profits and positive cash flow, but in effect, this is really the same as utilizing equity as, rather than distributing profits via issuing dividends, the company can elect to invest the excess earnings back into or inside the business. Further, larger and stronger companies can often leverage suppliers (by requesting extended credit terms) or customers (requiring deposits or enticing quicker payments) to "mine" cash or capital from key relationships. However, this just represents using a different type of debt as compared to formally structured and documented lending agreements. A perfect example of this is Tesla, which for years has required customers to provide a deposit or down payment in advance of finalizing the purchase of a car (which may take three to six months).

For the purposes of this chapter, we are going to focus our discussion on securing capital from external equity and debt sources as when large amounts of capital are required (relatively speaking to the size of the business), companies need to look to external capital sources such as banks, alternative lenders (an extremely broad group), venture capitalists, private equity groups, hedge funds, and, yes, Wall Street.

Equity

When best to utilize: Raising equity amounts to nothing more than selling a portion of the business to an external party that will own X% of the business moving forward (and have the right to future earnings). Equity sources of capital are best utilized when a company is operating in a higher-risk environment (e.g., new start-up operations or financing high growth), incurring losses, and/or needs to maintain a proper debt-to-equity balance (to avoid becoming overleveraged).

In our sample company, a decision was made to sell 500,000 shares of preferred equity to an outside party for $8 million (refer to Exhibit 9.1). The 500,000 shares amount to a 33.33% (500,000 shares divided by the total common and preferred shares of 1,500,000) ownership stake in the company, assuming all the preferred shares have the same basic rights to earnings as the common shares. The company elected to raise equity to help strengthen the balance sheet as well as to finance a large and potentially risky investment in an acquisition that cost $12.5 million.

We expand our discussion on raising equity capital in Chapter 17 and dive into the extremely important concepts of business control (what management influence will the equity investors have?) and ownership preferences (does their equity investment have a preference to earnings and company assets?) at this point.

 In summary, the pros of raising equity capital are centered in securing much-needed cash, strengthening the balance sheet, and potentially bringing on a valuable long-term capital and strategic partners (again, covered in Chapter 17), among others. The primary cons are centered in having to sell a portion of the company, diluting the current shareholder's ownership stake (in our example, diluting ownership from 100% to 66.67%) and possibly relinquishing certain management control over critical business decision-making activity.

Debt

When best to utilize: Raising debt is nothing more than securing a loan from a financial institution (e.g., bank, asset-based lender, risk-based lenders, etc.) that has set repayment terms and performance requirements. Debt sources of capital are best utilized when a company has assets available to pledge as collateral, can document and support that internal cash flows are adequate to service the debt, has enough strength in the balance sheet to avoid being overleveraged, and for companies that are relatively mature (with stable operations and proven profitability or a defendable path to profitability).

Referring to our sample company, it raised $8 million of debt in the form of a new loan to help finance the asset acquisition of $12.5 million. In total, our sample company raised $16 million of capital, 50% from equity and 50% from debt, to support the $12.5 million asset acquisition, leaving $3.5 million available for other purposes. You may ask why the company raised $16 million of capital when it needed just $12.5 million for the acquisition; the answer is simple. The company wanted to make sure it had additional equity capital to invest in new marketing and strategic growth initiatives that are anticipated to take additional time. Translation, it built a cushion to help navigate and manage potential hiccups to its business plan.

We expand our discussion on debt-based capital in the next section of this chapter but here we summarize the primary pros and cons of using debt capital.

The pros of utilizing debt capital are that it brings in much-needed cash, does not dilute the ownership of the existing investors (an extremely big pro), and helps reduce or limit the potential management influence that may be realized from bringing on new owners. The cons with utilizing debt capital are that the company will generally have to pledge assets as collateral (putting the assets at risk), must adhere to set loan repayment terms (committing future cash flows to repaying the debt), will have to pay interest on the loan, and will most likely have to abide by covenants established by the lender.

We should also note that various forms of capital are available that take on the characteristics of both debt and equity. A perfect example of this is what is commonly referred to as convertible debt (a form of a loan). Convertible debt has similar characteristics to the debt previously discussed but often has more flexible terms attached (e.g., specific assets do not need to be pledged as collateral) in exchange for having the option of converting into company equity if desired (based on a triggering event). Convertible debt is really just a form of equity capital in disguise, but it does offer significant benefits to both the issuing company and the party providing the loan, which we will discuss further in Chapter 17.

Finally, a quick word on other forms of capital, including technology, human, brand or market awareness, and similar types of nonfinancial capital. Needless to say, these are all critical forms of business capital and are essential to the success of any business but are beyond the scope of discussion for this book, as our goal is to keep you focused on understanding financial capital.

THE NATURE OF DEBT CAPITAL

We start our discussion on debt capital by overviewing some basic concepts, strategies, and terminologies to better help you understand debt-based capital at a more granular level. We then provide a more thorough overview of our sample company, the terms associated with the loan secured, and why it elected to utilize both debt and equity to finance its business plan.

> ➤ **Maturity and security:** To begin, always keep these two words in mind when thinking about debt – *maturity* and *security*. Maturity

means all debt must be repaid over an agreed-upon period based on the terms and interest rate established. Security refers to what assets are pledged and used as collateral or what type of guarantees are provided to support the loan.

➤ **Debt sources (i.e., loans):** There are literally hundreds of different types of financial institutions that are willing to provide loans. In fact, the innovation and evolution of lending sources over the past decade has been nothing short of amazing. But in the end, debt sources still generally fall into one of four primary groupings: traditional banks, risk-based lenders (a very broad group of financing sources, often referred to as shadow banking, that include asset-based lenders, hard money lenders, lenders disguised as companies providing "advances," and the list goes on and on), hybrid debt/equity lenders (e.g., convertible debt), and large financial institutions such as insurance companies (that may invest in the bonds issued by a public company).

To effectively raise debt capital, companies need to clearly understand where they stand in the lender risk appetite food chain. For stronger operating companies that have solid profits and financial strength, banks should be readily available to provide loans (and should also be the cheapest form of debt). For riskier companies that have shaky profits and are highly leveraged, the risk-based lenders would be more logical to approach given their appetite for these types of loans (which will also be far more expensive than banks'). And for the largest publicly traded companies, the public debt or bond markets should be accessible to raise capital (which can offer very inexpensive interest rates in the current environment).

➤ **Debt underwriting and costs:** The general rule is that when debt sources underwrite a loan, they first look to a company's ability to generate positive cash flow (to cover debt service payments), look to the value of the collateral second (in case the collateral needs to be liquidated to repay the loan), and finally, will rely on secondary repayment sources that generally fall outside of the company (e.g., a personal guarantee – PG – provided by an owner or a parent entity guarantee).

Also, it should be clear that the higher the perceived risk with issuing the loan the greater the return on the loan needs to be (to the parties providing the loan), which may come from higher interest rates, additional fees, or attaching some type of "equity kicker" (e.g., the loan includes an option or warrant to purchase X common shares at a discounted price if desired). However, a word of caution is warranted when raising debt capital as this ocean is filled with sharks, most of which are full of nasty surprises. You would be absolutely amazed at just how expensive debt can be when secured from the risk-based lenders, so do your homework and read the fine print as the devil is in the details.

➢ **Debt structure:** The balance sheet provides an important clue related to structuring loans correctly. If you refer to Exhibit 1.2, you will notice that the balance sheet presents the current portion of debt as a current liability and notes payable and other long-term debt as a long-term liability. This means that as of FYE 12/31/20, our sample company has $2 million of debt due within the next 12 months and approximately $6.6 million of long-term debt due past 12 months (in our case, over the next three years).

When securing debt-based capital, it is important to properly match long-term debt with assets that will generate profits and cash flow over a long-term period (e.g., five years) such as property, equipment, and intangible assets, as well as to match short-term sources of debt with current assets such as trade accounts receivable or inventory (that are anticipated to turn into cash relatively quickly). A perfect example of this strategy is securing a short-term loan, which is commonly referred to as a working capital line of credit, that uses a loan advance formula that varies with trade accounts receivable or inventory balances. Companies that have significant seasonality in their business cycles will structure a working capital line of credit that allows them to borrow up to 80% of eligible trade receivables (the collateral) to provide liquidity to support customer sales during the high season. As sales and trade accounts receivable increase, the company can borrow against the collateral to provide cash to support ongoing operations and then when the customers remit payment, the company has excess cash available, which it can then use to repay the line of credit lending facility. The key concept here is to properly match the structure of debt repayment term with the cash generation ability of the asset used as collateral.

➢ **Debt covenants:** Almost all loans will include lending covenants that provide guardrails (for lack of a better term) to ensure that a company maintains a certain financial performance to support the repayment of the loan. We covered some of these, including the debt service coverage ratio (DSCR) and loan-to-value (LTV) ratio, in Chapter 9, but it should also be mentioned that lenders will utilize a wide range of other covenants (financial and operational), including maintaining strong current ratios, establishing minimum profitability requirements (i.e., the company must generate positive earnings), requiring audited financial statements, and restricting the company from securing other loans, just to provide a few examples of other covenants.

The range of covenants is extensive and varies significantly by type of lender but the key for the borrower is to clearly understand their company's borrowing needs and market conditions to negotiate the covenants in advance (and as part of the loan underwriting process). For example, if you know that your company may have a soft year and struggle to break even, then avoiding a minimum profitability requirement covenant (at least for the year in question) would be advisable. You should use visibility of your company's financial performance from the forecasting process (covered in Chapter 10) to identify covenants that may be problematic, allowing you to negotiate more flexible and favorable covenants well in advance.

One final comment as it relates to covenants, as in the current economic environment and capital markets, you might come across the terms *cov.-lite* or *no-cov.* loans. These are just as they sound: cov.-lite means that a loan is being provided with noticeably light or low levels of covenants and no-cov. indicates that the loan basically has no covenants. Yes, we agree that it is nothing short of crazy for a lender to issue a loan with basically no covenants but then again, 2020 and 2021 are about some of the craziest markets we have ever seen.

OUR SAMPLE COMPANY'S FIRST YEAR PERFORMANCE – EYES OF THE LENDER

Please refer to Exhibits 1.3 and 9.1 to remind you that our sample company raised $16 million in new capital during FYE 12/31/20 to execute its business plan. Our sample company elected to use a combination of debt and equity by raising 50% in a new $8 million loan and $8 million in preferred equity. This balanced approach was utilized to avoid incurring excessive dilution, as if it had raised $16 million all in equity, it would have potentially released management control to the third-party investor (by providing a 50/50 ownership control of the company). If it had elected to raise $16 million of debt, the company might have overleveraged its operations and run the risk on defaulting on the loan (thus most likely triggering some very unpleasant conversations with the lenders). Hence, the company's executive management team and board of directors (which should provide approval) elected to strike a balance between debt and equity.

The company structured the debt facility with the following simplified terms. Note: In reality, the loan terms and conditions would be far more extensive but for ease of presentation, we have summarized just the key terms and conditions to drive home key concepts.

➢ Term: The loan is for a four-year period, with equal annual payments of $2 million due at the end of each year.

➢ Interest Rate: The loan carries an interest rate of 7.5% per annum. The interest rate reflects an elevated level of risk being absorbed by the lender to support an aggressive asset acquisition and pivot in the company's business interests.

➢ Senior or Secured Interest: For the lender to have a first secured interest in all company assets, the new loan required that the existing company debt, which amounted to $3 million (refer to Exhibit 1.3), be paid in full. The idea here is that the lender wants to make a senior position in all company assets (the collateral) to protect their loan.

➢ Covenants: The loan includes a debt service coverage ratio of 1.50:1.00 and that the company must maintain a tangible net worth ratio of no greater than 2.00:1.00.

➢ Preferred Dividends: If any covenant is violated or the company defaults on the loan, the issuance of preferred or common dividends is not allowed. This provision required the approval of the preferred investors.

➢ Additional Debt: No additional loans above $500,000 may be secured by the company without the approval of the lender.

Exhibit 13.1 presents our sample company's summarized income statement along with lender covenant ratio calculations for evaluation. Of particular interest should be the following items:

> ➤ *External financial statement format:* We would like to draw your attention to the summary version of the income statement, which has been tailored for external presentation to the lender. More than

EXHIBIT 13.1   Unaudited Debt Covenant Analysis and Summary Income Statement

Unaudited - Prepared by Company Management

QW Example Tech., Inc.
Unaudited Financial Statements
& Debt Covenant Analysis
For the Fiscal Year Ending
12/31/2020

Loan Covenants Review	Actual 12/31/2020	Planned 12/31/2020
Covenants Review, Lender:		
Debt Service Coverage Ratio, FYE:		
Net Income (Loss)	$2,913,821	$6,839,625
Interest Expense	$400,000	$425,000
Depreciation & Amortization Expense	$2,421,429	$2,400,000
Adjusted Debt Service Cash Flow	$5,735,250	$9,664,625
Interest Expense	$400,000	$425,000
Loan Principal Payments Due, 1 Yr.	$2,000,000	$2,000,000
Total Debt Service Payments, 1 Yr.	$2,400,000	$2,425,000
Debt Service Coverage Ratio	2.39	3.99
Debt to Tangible Net Equity Ratio, FYE:		
Total Liabilities	$16,586,750	$17,692,385
Total Owner's Equity	$21,904,536	$25,830,339
Less: Intangible Assets	($12,500,000)	($12,500,000)
Tangible Net Equity	$9,404,536	$13,330,339
Debt to Tangible Net Equity Ratio	1.76	1.33

The company is well in compliance with the lender DSCR of 1.50x but notice how far off it was from the original projection. The debt to tangible net worth ratio is also met but not near as much room is present with lender requirement of 2.0x.

Income Statement for the Fiscal Year Ending	Actual 12/31/2020	% of Net Rev.	Forecast 12/31/2020	% of Net Rev.
Sales Revenue:				
Net Sales Revenue	$72,198,250	100.00%	$77,300,000	100.00%
Costs of Goods Sold:				
Total Costs of Goods Sold	$27,541,000	38.15%	$27,425,000	35.48%
Gross Profit	$44,657,250	61.85%	$49,875,000	64.52%
Gross Margin	61.85%		64.52%	
Corporate Expenses & Overhead:				
Direct Operating Expenses	$17,435,600	24.15%	$17,500,000	22.64%
Corporate Marketing, Branding, & Promotional	$2,671,400	3.70%	$2,500,000	3.23%
Research, Development, & Design	$12,996,000	18.00%	$13,527,500	17.50%
Corporate Overhead & Support	$2,250,000	3.12%	$2,500,000	3.23%
Depreciation & Amortization Expense	$2,421,429	3.35%	$2,400,000	3.10%
Total Operating Expenses	$37,774,429	52.32%	$38,427,500	49.71%
Operating Income (EBIT)	$6,882,821	9.53%	$11,447,500	14.81%
Operating Margin (EBIT Margin)	9.53%		14.81%	
Other Expenses (Income):				
Other Expenses, Income, & Discontinued Ops.	$2,000,000	2.77%	$500,000	0.65%
Interest Expense	$400,000	0.55%	$425,000	0.55%
Total Other Expenses (Income)	$2,400,000	3.32%	$925,000	1.20%
Net Income (Loss) Before Taxes	$4,482,821	6.21%	$10,522,500	13.61%
Income Tax Expense (Benefit)	$1,569,000	2.17%	$3,682,875	4.76%
Net Income (Loss) After Taxes	$2,913,821	4.04%	$6,839,625	8.85%

Notice the summary version of the financial statement format which is used for external presentation purposes to the lender. A bit more info. is provided but not at the same level as the internal financial statements.

Confidential - Property of QW Example Tech., Inc.

likely, a balance sheet and statement of cash flows would also be presented but in an external format. Lenders, like other external parties, need to only receive the properly formatted and presented financial information.

➤ ***Forecasts:*** When the company secured the $8 million from the lender, it presented forecast operating results for FYE 12/31/20, which is what the lender used to underwrite the loan (along with historical operating results). As you can see from both the comparison income statements and covenant ratio calculations, our sample company's actual FYE 12/31/20 financial performance is considerably lower than the forecasts. The negative performance with sales revenue will definitely be a focal point, as it has the single biggest impact on the reduction to the company's bottom line.

➤ ***Covenant compliance:*** Our sample company is still in compliance with the loan covenants established of 1.50x for the DSCR and 2.00x for the debt-to-tangible-net-worth ratio. It would appear that the company negotiated covenants that provided a reasonable amount of cushion in the event it did not achieve forecasts (which was clearly the case). So, kudos to the company for having the foresight to build plenty of cushion in the covenants but a word of warning as another down or difficult year and the company may blow through (a term used when a business violates a covenant) the debt-to-tangible-net-worth ratio.

In summary, our sample company will more than likely have some explaining to do with the lender, as the trending with the financial performance and loan covenant ratios are all negative. The company's management team will need to make sure it has a complete understanding of the current year operating results, what went right and what did not, and relay confidence in future year forecasts and that the loan is on solid footing. The ability to communicate, with confidence, a strong outlook and economic story for the company will be extremely important as the management team meets with both the lender and preferred equity investors, both new parties that combined invested $16 million in the business over the past 12 months.

CHAPTER 14

Net Profits and Cash Flow – Real or Imaginary?

LET'S START WITH THE OBVIOUS

Introductory courses in business or economics 101 generally start by introducing principles or concepts that are universal in nature, simple to understand, and extremely important. In economics 101, the concept is supply and demand; that is, higher supply combined with lower demand results in falling prices and vice versa when supply is constrained and demand is high. For business 101, the simple concept is that all companies must generate a profit to remain in business – translation, annual sales revenue is greater than annual expenses, equating to being able to generate an annual profit.

Seems simple enough but in today's economic environment, the public equity markets continue to provide opportunities for companies like Uber Technologies, Inc. (aka Uber) to remain in business even though they consume hefty amounts of cash and generate large losses. Can this go on forever? Probably not (unless of course you are the United States government, which racks up huge deficits and debt that will most likely never be repaid), but when public equity markets are operating in an optimistic mindset, companies like Uber can continue to raise capital (i.e., cash) in hopes of eventually being profitable. Unfortunately, most companies cannot operate like Uber and absorb years of losses that are covered by round after round of financing. Yes, they exist, but no, that is not the real world.

In Chapter 13, we covered the topic of capitalizing a business (i.e., it takes money to make money), while Chapters 15 and 16 will dive into the concepts of valuing a business and the basics of business acquisitions (how much is the baked cake worth?). Chapter 14 focuses on the profit-making activities of a business to help understand what is real versus imaginary. Or to make this even easier to understand, what is the bottom line, what capital was required to support the business model, and what is it worth? Make, take, and bake: How much (profit) did you make, how much (capital) did it take, and yes, how much (the business) is the baked cake worth?

We should note that seldom does a newly launched business (or operating unit) generate a net profit right out of the gate. It usually takes a considerable amount of time to create a business plan, launch the business, develop markets, and deliver reliable products (or services) in ample volume to cover all expenses and to generate a profit. This is generally the rule rather than the exception and kudos to those businesses that can generate real profits out of the gate, but rarely, and we mean rarely, is this the case. Companies must grow, adapt, and adjust their business models over a period of time to eventually reach profitability that can be delivered in a reliable, year-over-year fashion. The balance of this chapter focuses on profit-generating strategies, both real and "illusional," that companies utilize to improve profitability.

FIXED, VARIABLE, AND SEMI-VARIABLE EXPENSES

The next section of this chapter delves into a deeper analysis of how companies make various business decisions to improve profitability. But before we discuss various profit-making strategies, a quick refresher course is warranted on the three primary types of expense a business incurs – fixed, variable, and semi-variable.

1. *Fixed:* Fixed expenses represent costs that are fixed, set, or firm over an extended period of time (e.g., a year or more) and are often referred to as period expenses. A perfect example of a fixed expense would be a lease for a building that requires a company to pay $10,000 a month for the next 60 months (representing a five-year lease), regardless of how much sales the company generates or profits it earns. Depreciation expense is another example of a period or fixed expense, as if a company has a $1,000,000 asset and depreciates this asset over 60 months, each month the company will record depreciation expense

of $16,667. Further examples of fixed costs include subscription or technology support contracts that may run a year or longer and wages paid to company executives that may have a long-term guaranteed employment agreement.

2. *Variable:* Variable expenses represent costs that vary directly with sales revenue levels based either on the number of units sold or the price realized. For example, an ecommerce retailer that sells clothing should know that for each pair of a specific type of shoe sold, the cost of each pair is $12. So, if 100 pairs of shoes are sold, $1,200 of expense is incurred and if zero pairs of shoes are sold, $0 of expense is incurred. It is important to note that the variable nature of expenses is not related to unit volume alone, as some expenses are associated with price and not volume. An example of this would be merchant fees paid to credit card processing companies that charge 2.5% of every dollar a company receives from credit card sales.

3. *Semi-variable:* It should come as no surprise that semi-variable expenses are costs that over the short term (e.g., 90 days or less) are fixed in nature but over the medium or longer term can be increased or decreased, with some degree of proactive control by company management as business conditions dictate. Regular employee wages and burden (e.g., payroll taxes, health insurance, etc.) provide an example of this, as a company may establish a staff level of 10 full-time employees operating in a customer support and service function based on an anticipated sales range of $3 million to $5 million over a 90-day period. The company may commit to this staffing level for the first 90 days and then adjust their headcount based on actual sales revenue achieved and revised outlooks.

Smart businesses realize that it is just as important to understand business expenses by function, that is, costs of goods sold or costs of sales, direct operating expenses, corporate overhead, general and administrative, and other expenses (which is how expenses are presented in the income statement) versus the type of expenses in relation to being fixed, variable, or semi-variable. This allows companies the ability to adjust operations and pivot or adapt quickly to changing business conditions, cutting expenses when needed and adding expenses if warranted.

GENERATING REAL PROFITS

We now turn our attention to understanding the business economics of attempting to improve profits via driving the top-line sales (which is not as easy as simply increasing sales to increase profits). As will be clear in the example, there are situations in which driving higher sales can lead to increased losses.

Exhibit 14.1 provides a simple example of an ecommerce company attempting to drive top-line sales to increase operating profits via increased sales price (scenario #3) compared to increased sales volume (scenario #2). This exhibit also presents a summarized income statement that incorporates the concept of understanding fixed, variable, and semi-variable expenses.

What do the results in our analysis tell us? Well, here is the long and short of it for our ecommerce company asking the question whether they should drive sales or profits:

> ➤ Scenario 1 displays a company that can generate a reasonable operating profit of roughly $202,000 on approximately $7.5 million of sales revenue – not a horrible performance, but something management would like to improve on, as a 4.28% operating margin is not going to cut it with the investors (as well as the industry standard being closer to 10%). Please also note that the company's corporate overhead or fixed annual costs are expected to remain at $1.5 million under all the scenarios. This is due to the fact that the company's corporate infrastructure has been designed to support annual sales levels ranging from $5 to $10 million.

> ➤ Scenario 2 presents a scenario where unit sales volumes are increased by 10% but this comes at a significant cost, as not only is the average selling price reduced from $215 to $204 (as more aggressive discounting is required to sell more units), but higher direct selling expenses (i.e., advertising and commissions) are incurred to push 10% more units out the door. The result speaks for itself because even though the company increased top-line sales, it swung from an operating profit to an operating loss via the increased direct selling expenses combined with the lower net sales price per unit. This scenario also highlights the impact of variable unit costs remaining the same at $75 per unit

EXHIBIT 14.1   DTC Business Unaudited Sales Profitability Comparison

Unaudited - Prepared by Company Management

XYZ DtoC Example, Inc.
Profitability Comparison
as of the Fiscal Year Ending
12/31/2020

Description	Scenario 1 Amount	% of Sales	Scenario 2 Amount	% of Sales	Scenario 3 Amount	% of Sales
Selling KPIs, Annual:						
Number of Units Sold	35,000		38,500		31,500	
Average Selling Price	$215		$204		$226	
Average Cost of Unit, Fully Loaded	$75		$75		$75	
Average Merchant Fee, % of Sales	2.50%		2.50%		2.50%	
Average Direct Selling Expense, Adv. & Comm.	40.00%		42.00%		38.00%	
Summary Income Statement, Annual:						
Sales Revenue	$7,525,000	100.00%	$7,863,625	100.00%	$7,111,125	100.00%
Costs of Goods Sold, Unit	($2,625,000)	-34.88%	($2,887,500)	-36.72%	($2,362,500)	-33.22%
Costs of Sales, Merchant Fee	($188,125)	-2.50%	($196,591)	-2.50%	($177,778)	-2.50%
Gross Profit	$4,711,875	62.62%	$4,779,534	60.78%	$4,570,847	64.28%
Gross Margin	62.62%		60.78%		64.28%	
Direct Selling Expenses, Advertising & Commissions	$3,010,000	40.00%	$3,302,723	42.00%	$2,702,228	38.00%
Corporate Overhead (fixed costs)	$1,500,000	19.93%	$1,500,000	19.08%	$1,500,000	21.09%
Operating Profit (EBITDA)	$201,875	2.68%	($23,188)	-0.29%	$368,619	5.18%
Operating Margin (EBITDA Margin)	4.28%		-0.49%		8.06%	

Confidential - Property of XYZ DtoC Example, Inc.

but, with a lower average sales price, the company's gross margin decreases from 62.6% to 60.8%.

➢ And our surprise is in scenario 3 as, even with lower top-line sales revenue, the company was able to generate a higher gross margin, which when combined with lower direct selling expenses and a static fixed cost structure, an operating profit of roughly $370,000 is achieved, amounting to an operating margin of 8.06% (more in line with industry standards). Of particular importance is that the company's direct selling expenses for advertising and commissions decreased to 38% from 42% (in scenario 2). This was achieved through proactively reducing semi-variable advertising and commission expenses by eliminating ineffective advertising and unproductive sales representatives.

This growth-at-all-costs mentality can really get investors excited, but what begins to become apparent very quickly is that chasing incremental sales by targeting weaker customers with more aggressive selling strategies will generally lead to increased losses, higher cash burn rates, and the need for ever more financial capital to stay afloat.

 The reason this example was provided is to highlight a common trap or mistake companies make with their business models. That is, companies will often try to impress investors by highlighting rapid sales growth without paying attention to the bottom line. They do this in an attempt to attract investors and raise capital by basically relaying the message of "look how fast we're growing so you'd better get on the bandwagon" as well as "don't worry about profits as these will come down the road as the business matures" – translation, we will grow our way into profits (which of course does not make any sense, as for each incremental unit sale, the company is actually losing more money).

Exhibit 14.2 provides a second perspective on how operating profits can be increased, even though direct costs of sales have increased and the company's gross margin has decreased. Our example this time is presented for a professional service company that bills out its staff on various consulting projects.

Here again, we highlight the key outputs on why this company would be willing to operate with an overall lower gross margin (decreasing

EXHIBIT 14.2 Example Small Company Unaudited Profitability Comparison

Unaudited - Prepared by Company Management

Local Sample Service Co, Inc.
Profitability Comparison
as of the Fiscal Year Ending
12/31/2020

Description	Scenario 1 Amount	% of Sales	Scenario 2 Amount	% of Sales	Variance Amount
Selling KPIs, Annual:					
Hours of Staff Time Billed	33,280		46,592		13,312
Average Hourly Bill Rate	$200		$175		($25)
Average Hourly Staff Cost, Fully Burdened	$125		$114		$11
Direct Operating & Account Mgmt. Expenses	10.00%		9.00%		1.00%
Summary Income Statement, Annual:					
Sales Revenue	$6,656,000	100.00%	$8,153,600	100.00%	$1,497,600
Costs of Sales, Staff Wages & Burden	($4,160,000)	-62.50%	($5,294,545)	-64.94%	($1,134,545)
Gross Profit	$2,496,000	37.50%	$2,859,055	35.06%	$363,055
Gross Margin	37.50%		35.06%		24.24%
Direct Operating & Account Mgmt. Expenses	$665,600	10.00%	$733,824	9.00%	($68,224)
Corporate Overhead (fixed costs)	$1,500,000	22.54%	$1,500,000	18.40%	$0
Operating Profit (EBITDA)	$330,400	4.96%	$625,231	7.67%	$294,831
Operating Margin (EBITDA Margin)	13.24%		21.87%		8.63%

Confidential - Property of Local Sample Service Co, Inc.

from 37.5% to 35.06%) for the benefit of increasing top-line sales and operating profits:

➤ Note that the company's average bill rate decreased from $200 per hour to $175 per hour but at the same time, the company was able to secure large new consulting projects, enabling it to increase annual billable hours by 13,312. Further, the average hourly fully burdened staff cost (which includes wages, payroll taxes, insurance, training, paid time off, etc.) decreased from $125 to $114. This decrease did not come from paying employees less; rather, the company realized that by taking on additional consulting projects, the staff's productivity level would increase by 7.5% (i.e., the company is able to keep their staff busier and bill more hours of work). Translation, the staff is being managed and billed to jobs more efficiently.

➢ Another key to the company's improved operating performance is that direct operating and corporate overhead expenses only increased slightly between the scenarios (by roughly $68,000). The reason for this is centered in the fact that the company realized that it had adequate infrastructure established to support the increase in sales, thus spreading more sales revenue over a relatively constant expense structure. Even though the incremental gross margin for the increase in business amounted to only 24.24%, through leveraging fixed expenses more efficiently, the company was able to improve annual operating profits by $295,000 and increase its operating margin from 13.24% to 21.87%.

A key concept brought to light in Exhibit 14.2 is the theory of economies of scale; that is, when a company has made a fixed investment in infrastructure or capital assets, it should be able to gain efficiencies by utilizing or leveraging the fixed investment more efficiently with marginal increases in sales. Economies of scale really takes hold in manufacturing companies, considering how significant certain period or fixed expenses can be, such as building leases or equipment depreciation. If a manufacturing company can increase production (and sales) by 25% but its fixed expenses remain largely the same, in effect what the company has achieved is the ability to spread higher sales volumes of the same expense level, which should drive higher profits (assuming the ultimate sales price is adequate to cover variable product costs).

We could provide countless additional examples of how companies evaluate business opportunities to improve operating profits, but close this section by highlighting three critical concepts. First, we harp on the concept of completeness yet again (yes, we know this is getting old), as focusing on only one line item of operating results can be dangerous (e.g., top-line sales revenue). When completing profitability analyses, understanding the impact on sales is just the start of the food chain as flowing the analysis through gross profits and operating profits is even more important.

Second, having a clear understanding of the three primary expense types of variable, fixed, and semi-variable, and how these expenses relate to both volume and price changes, is essential. And third, improving real profits should end up driving real cash flow and thus improve the real value of a business. No accounting or financial gimmickry here as the goal is to ensure that sound economic business decisions can be made to increase real profits and cash.

MANUFACTURING IMAGINARY PROFITS

We start this section by referring you back to Chapter 12, where the concept of financial engineering was discussed, and take this opportunity to expand on how profits can be "manufactured" by using accounting strategies (which contrasts with the previous section, where we discussed generating real profits and cash flow). We would also like to be perfectly clear that the content provided in this section should not be confused with accounting or financial fraud. Rather, the concepts highlighted below originate from companies adjusting or changing specific accounting policies, procedures, use of estimates, and so on over several years as business conditions or operating circumstances change. These are legitimate (per GAAP) but warrant a closer look by both internal and external parties when companies move down this path. We have provided four examples for you to chew (or maybe the more appropriate word would be *gag*) on:

1. ***Change in estimate:*** Chapter 7 provided insight into a company's investment cycle, including selecting appropriate depreciation, amortization, or depletion estimates (to appropriately expense the consumption of an asset over a period of time). Companies may elect to revise these estimates based on changes to their operating environment. For example, if an asset was originally anticipated to be fully consumed and depreciated over a five-year period but based on revised management estimates that indicate the asset has a longer life the life was extended to seven years, then the period depreciation expense would naturally decrease, as the asset would be depreciated over a longer period. The same logic could be used when amortizing intellectual property, but the point is that a simple change in an estimate from, say, five years to seven could impact operating performance significantly. Other examples would be a company changing an estimate for potential sales returns or future warranty-related costs as they

"scrub" operating results to be more accurate. We will let you decide if a company scrubbing operating results is doing so legitimately or to achieve a specific performance target, but as we noted in Chapter 5, accounting estimates is always an area that should demand attention.

2. ***Change in policy:*** A change in accounting estimate should not be confused with a change in accounting policy. For example, a company may change its policy related to capitalizing assets on the balance sheet versus expensing costs in the income statement. Research and development costs that were expensed historically may now be capitalized as an intangible asset and amortized over an appropriate period (as management has determined that the R&D costs are a valuable long-term asset). In either case, cash still flows out the door, but companies may want to "park" the capitalized asset on the balance sheet and then depreciate or amortize the asset over a period of time, helping improve the income statement.

3. ***Interest rates:*** Interest rates are currently at historical lows (and some would say they are artificially low, manipulated by the Federal Reserve Bank). Chapter 15 dives into the topic of valuing businesses and the impact low interest rates have on propping up business valuations. The same logic applies to specific assets such as intellectual property or proprietary content that will generate future cash flows. In effect, low interest rates prop up asset values by discounting the future cash flow at a low rate (which increases the future value of the asset). Companies may attempt to justify using lower interest rates to support a higher asset value and avoid writing off the asset or having to expense the asset over a shorter period.

4. ***Cleaning house:*** The three previous examples focused on how a company may inflate operating profits and earnings. The concept of cleaning house does the exact opposite, as a common strategy companies use when bad news needs to be delivered (to the market or investors) is to deliver all the bad news at once. Or, simply put, let us clean house with all potential write-offs, adjustments, losses, and so on in one time period to sacrifice the current year to build a clean basis to drive profits in future years. Mind you, no cash changes hands with these types of events; rather, the balance sheet is simply adjusted to eliminate the crap on the balance sheet (e.g., worthless inventory, unsupportable assets, quickly fading IP/content, etc.). If you refer back to our sample company and its story, a similar cleaning house strategy was used but in a slightly different fashion. You will notice a

large decrease in the inventory value as of FYE 12/31/20 compared to FYE 12/31/19, dropping from $4.3 million to $1.8 million. You might also note an "other expense" of $2 million in FYE 12/31/20 (which, for your benefit, includes writing off worthless inventory of $1 million). For the company to stay profitable each year, (for whatever reason) management elected to write off the inventory and record the adjustment during FYE 12/31/20 when higher profits were present (to absorb the hit). Further, management concluded that this represents a one-time expense from a discontinued product line that will be nonrecurring (thus the reason it is captured below the operating income or EBITDA line).

We would like to emphasize two important points as they relate to manufacturing profits. First, in the four examples provided above, no cash changes hands. None, zero, zip! This is to say that the losses are not real, as somewhere in the past cash was impacted by either investing in a long-term asset or buying inventory (to provide two examples). Yes, the losses are very much real and the company's management team needs to be held accountable for any performance issues. But the adjustments noted above represent somewhat of a sleight of accounting hand to move expenses or costs between the balance sheet and income statement in a manner that is, for lack of a better term, desirable (to achieve certain goals or confirm a story).

Second, there is nothing inherently wrong with these strategies, especially when a company's external CPA auditor has agreed to the changes and confirms that the changes comply with GAAP. But you should always watch for these items in relation to the size of adjustments, the frequency, and the reasoning/validity, as they may indicate either a management effort to "massage" the financial results or, worse yet, weaknesses in the company's internal accounting system and financial information reporting.

CASH FLOW AS OUR VALIDATION

So here we are again, and no doubt beating a dead horse. That is, understand the income statement, trust the balance sheet, and, most importantly, rely on the statement of cash flows. Given the amount of leeway companies have with preparing the balance sheet and income statement, the statement of cash flows can help root out inconsistencies or peculiarities in a company's financial results by following the flow of cash. In a sense, the statement of cash flows acts as a de facto audit mechanism to help validate the economic viability of the business.

You may hear statements from time to time such as "in the black but where's the green," which refers to a company generating a profit but experiencing cash flow difficulties (i.e., not having enough greenbacks or dollars). This may be fully explainable and perfectly normal for a high-growth business that is consuming large amounts of capital and internal earnings to finance growth. But the company's operating story, financial statements, reports, and financial information should all be aligned in a manner that makes sense, as when financial imbalances arise, they can usually be traced directly to a company's ability to generate positive cash flows.

CHAPTER 15

Business Valuations – Why and How?

WHY VALUE A BUSINESS?

Let us start with the first and most relevant question: Why are business valuations even necessary? Basically, it comes down to one of the following four primary reasons:

1. **Liquidity event:** It should be relatively obvious that for most (but not all) business there comes a time to achieve a liquidity or exit event (clever names for selling the business). Although companies can achieve a liquidity event through undertaking an initial public offering (i.e., IPO) on a large stock exchange such as Nasdaq, this is generally reserved for the largest multibillion-dollar organizations. For most smaller businesses that generate annual sales measured in millions of dollars, outright sales of a business are usually more effective strategies to achieve a liquidity event.

   The motivations for business sales vary and may arise for any number of reasons, including business partners wanting to be bought out, early investors looking to cash out, a family-owned business that has reached the end of the line (i.e., no further heirs left to operate the business), a group of employees wants to buy the business from the founders, or a change in market conditions necessitates the sale of a business, to name a few. To achieve a fair and equitable sale of a business, a proper valuation must be established.

2. ***Raising capital:*** As discussed in Chapter 13 (capitalizing a business), companies frequently must raise capital to finance ongoing operations and often do this through selling equity. Whether this is done at the private level (e.g., a venture capitalist firm investing in a new technology start-up) or at the public level (e.g., a company undertakes an initial public offering or IPO to raise capital in the public markets), the same concept holds. That is, X% of the company is sold for $Y, which is dependent on a business value being set. You would never simply invest $Y not knowing how much of a company you would own, thus the reason for setting the valuation.

    It should also be noted that even when a business raises debt to help finance operations, a business valuation may be required. A perfect example of this is with real estate, as a lending institution may require an appraisal (or valuation) to be completed prior to extending a loan. This is a topic we discussed in Chapter 9 related to the loan-to-value ratio.

3. ***Business planning and risk management:*** Valuations are also extremely helpful in assisting with the management of the business as it relates to supporting various tasks such as ensuring that proper levels of insurance are secured (to protect company assets), establishing benchmarks to evaluate the progress of a business, helping set values for potential equity participation or incentive plans (extended to the companies employees), assisting with evaluating potential business tax obligations or assessments (if business legal forms are changed), and various other management functions.

4. ***Estate and personal planning:*** Valuations are integral and an essential part of the personal financial planning and management process, ranging from estates to gifting to potential marriage dilutions (which all involve protecting accumulated wealth and managing potential taxes that may arise). Estate planning is currently a significant focus area as not only is a massive transfer of wealth about to occur as the Baby Boomers retire and expire (sorry, we all have an expiration date) but, in addition, political winds changed in 2020, favoring a much more aggressive position being taken by the U.S. government on levying additional taxes on the wealthy. Increased taxes on the wealthy were a basis of the Democrats' campaign strategy in 2020 and will almost certainly be enacted by 2022. For high-net-worth individuals and families, several of whom own all or a portion

of businesses, the need to establish a fair value for these businesses represents a critical element of their estate planning process.

We might offer one final comment or thought on a business valuation as it relates to its need or purpose. In the case of valuing a business for a company sale or to raise capital, the primary objective is usually to drive the valuation as high as possible. On the flipside, when businesses are valued for estate taxation purposes or to potentially buy out a pain-in-the-ass partner, lower business valuations may be desired to help reduce potential estate taxes or decrease the amount paid to an exiting partner.

If you recall from Chapter 5, a reference was made to accounting being more of an art form than a science. The same concept holds with estimating business values as there is no question that the desired result or objective will often influence and dictate the final valuation. Or thinking of it in simpler terms and as the old accounting adage goes, "What does two-plus-two equal?" to which the accountant replies, "What does it need to be?"

HOW TO VALUE A BUSINESS?

To keep this as simple as possible, all business valuations, in one fashion or another, are based on two key variables: number one, the ability to generate positive cash flows (or profits), and number two, the discount rate applied to future cash flows. No matter what valuation model, methodology, logic, concept, technique, and/or principle is used, they all come back to the company's ability to generate future positive cash flow and then discount that cash flow back to "today" to calculate a value. Even when a company is being liquidated, the end value is based on how much cash will be left over for the equity owners after all assets have been liquidated and debts paid. Simply put, cash flow reigns as king when valuing a business.

Throughout this book, we have covered the income statement, profit generation, and cash flows (the first of the two key variables) extensively. We will revisit the cash flow side of the equation later in this chapter but at this point, it is important that you understand the second key variable, which is based in the universal concept involving the time value of money (the present value of future cash flows or discounted cash flows). Simply stated, the *time value of money concept* assumes that a dollar in your hand today is worth more than a dollar in your hand next year, two years from today, and so on. Looking back a couple of decades, when interest rates were north of 5% and the Federal Reserve Bank had not stepped in to drive interest rates to close to 0%, the impact of the time value of money was much more pronounced than it is today. Exhibit 15.1 shows an example that highlights just how impactful low interest rates can be on a business value.

EXHIBIT 15.1   DTC Business Unaudited Company Valuation Comparison

Unaudited - Prepared by Company Management

XYZ DtoC Example, Inc.
Estimated Company Value – Comparison
as of the Fiscal Year Ending
12/31/2020

Summary Income Statement – EBITDA	FYE	Amount $
EBITDA, Actual FYE	12/31/2020	$1,500,000
EBITDA, Forecast FYE	12/31/2021	$1,800,000
EBITDA, Forecast FYE	12/31/2022	$2,160,000
EBITDA, Forecast FYE	12/31/2023	$2,592,000
EBITDA, Forecast FYE	12/31/2024	$3,110,400
EBITDA, Forecast FYE	12/31/2025	$3,732,480
EBITDA, Forecast FYE	12/31/2026	$4,478,976
EBITDA, Forecast FYE	12/31/2027	$5,374,771
EBITDA, Forecast FYE	12/31/2028	$6,449,725
EBITDA, Forecast FYE	12/31/2029	$7,739,671
Net Present Value of Cash Flow Stream @	**4.00%**	$29,839,831
Net Present Value of Cash Flow Stream @	**8.00%**	$23,349,650
Change in Value based on Discount Rate		21.75%

Confidential - Property of XYZ DtoC Example, Inc.

Exhibit 15.1 calculates the value of a business assuming a starting point of $1.5 million in annual EBITDA/cash flow, which is forecast to grow for the next nine years at a 20% compounded growth rate. Assuming a 4% discount rate, the company's value is estimated to be roughly $30 million. Apply an 8% discount rate to the same cash flow stream and the value decreases to roughly $23.3 million (a 21.75% decrease).

It should be noted that there are countless business valuation metrics in use today that are generally driven by key operating performance standards or targets as established within different industries. For example, the real estate industry bases most valuations on a property's NOI (net operating income) divided by a cap rate – translation, the net operating income or operating profit (i.e., cash flow) divided by a capitalization rate (i.e., discount rate). Another example that is relevant in today's economy is how SaaS companies are valued. For those not familiar with this term, SaaS stands for software as a service and is related to technology companies that sell subscription software services (e.g., Shopify, Slack, etc.) to customers who repeatedly use the technology year in and year out. Quite often, these companies are valued by applying a valuation multiple on the company's ARR (annual recurring revenue). For example, if a company generates $30 million a year in ARR and receives a 5x multiple on this figure, the company would be valued at $150 million. Again, here is the translation: What most investors know is that a company that produces $30 million a year in SaaS ARR should be able to generate operating profits (positive cash flow) of 25% or more on this revenue or $7.5 million. So basically, the valuation has been set at 20x operating profits, which backs into a discount rate of approximately 4.5% (assuming no change in annual operating profits of $7.5 million for a time period of 50 years). The 4.5% discount rate may appear low, but in this case an investor may be "banking" on the company achieving above-average revenue and operating profit growth rates, translating into higher future positive cash flows.

Countless models exist to value businesses and can get to be complex (especially when the Wall Street financial wizards get involved). However, two valuation techniques are particularly common and the easiest to understand are summarized below.

1. *Cash flow multiple method:* This method is applicable to most small to medium-sized business operations and is often referred to as the Main Street approach. Under this method, a cash flow multiple is applied to a company's expected/future adjusted cash flow stream. This adjusted cash flow stream is commonly referred to as EBITDA (which has been covered in numerous chapters in this book). Cash flow multiples often range from a low end of 3 to over 20 and are influenced by a company's perceived risk and growth factors. In addition, it should be noted that historical cash flow information tends to be used as a basis or starting point when calculating the expected/future "adjusted" cash flow stream. For example, if a company's prior-year

EBITDA was $1,500,000 annually and a multiple of 8 is applied, the business's value is approximately $12,000,000 ($1,500,000 × 8). This business valuation method is more widely utilized by Main Street than the price–earnings multiple method due to the nature of how these companies operate (a high volume of relatively small and unsophisticated businesses compared to corporate America as represented by Wall Street).

EBITDA stands for earnings before interest, taxes, depreciation, and amortization. EBITDA represents the basis for determining a business's adjusted cash flow on which to base a business valuation. In addition, this term can be expanded to *EBITDA&O,* which simply adds the term *other* to the end. Several businesses need to add other expenses to this equation to account for various one-time or owner preference expenses and income that are nonrecurring in nature. By accounting for these one-time and nonrecurring items, the calculation of a company's adjusted cash flow stream can be clearly supported (EBITDA updated for other expenses and income that are nonrecurring in nature).

To further your understanding of EBITDA and why it is used, business valuations tend to be based on a company's ability to generate real or comparable operating income and cash flows (between similar companies operating in similar markets). The idea is to identify how much cash flow can be generated from the basic business operation as opposed to how much debt the business has incurred (producing interest expense) and how much has been invested in fixed assets (producing depreciation expense) to support the business. As an example, interest expense is added back to account for the fact that similar businesses may have been financed differently (one using debt and another using equity). While one of the businesses would have interest expense that would produce lower net profits, the other would not, producing higher profits. External business valuations need to extract the impact of how a company has been financed to properly calculate a real value for the assets being acquired. After the real value has been determined, the parties can then structure how best to finance the potential acquisition.

2. ***Price-Earnings Multiple Method:*** This method is most applicable to larger, publicly traded businesses and is often referred to as the Wall Street approach. Using this technique, a business valuation is derived from taking the net after-tax profit of a company and multiplying it by a market-driven factor. For companies that enjoy the prospects

of high growth rates, dominant market positions, significant financial resources, and other positive business attributes – all of which translate into potential significant higher future cash flow streams – a multiple of 20 or more may be applied (and extreme cases of over 100 for companies such as Tesla or Amazon). For businesses that are more mature with relatively steady cash flow streams, a lower multiple, such as 12 to 15, may be applied. This is one (but certainly not the only) reason why a company such as Microsoft may be valued using a factor of 36 whereas a food company such as Conagra may be valued using a factor of only 18. This technique is most prevalent with publicly traded companies listed on the New York Stock Exchange, Nasdaq, and other markets. The market quickly and efficiently establishes the total value of the company (its market capitalization) that is readily available at any point in time.

Exhibit 15.2 presents three valuation scenarios for the same company but incorporating three different (and critical) valuation drivers. For simplicity, we calculated the values by discounting cash flows for only a 10-year period (as opposed to discounting cash flows over an extended period of 30 years).

The first is the assumed future annual growth rate in earnings (or EBITDA), which starts at 8% in scenario 1 and increases to 16% in scenario 3. The second is the discount rate applied to future cash flows, which starts at a high of 12% in scenario 1 and decreases to 6% in scenario 3. And third, notice that the adjusted EBITDA figure in scenario 3 is $1.8 million compared to the actual EBITDA figure of $1.5 million in scenarios 1 and 2.

How did the EBITDA figure magically increase by $300,000 or 20%? Simple – addbacks! The company is going to attempt to convince an external party that there is really an extra $300,000 of internal earnings when various expense addbacks are accounted for (i.e., expenses that would not be present moving forward but were incurred in FYE 12/31/20). These addbacks may range from excessive owner compensation to one-time expenses (that will be nonrecurring) to employee reductions because of eliminating duplicate functions to you name it, as the creativity, imagination, and storytelling (i.e., usually fictional stories, we might add) displayed when calculating addbacks can definitely be worthy of an Oscar for the best visual effects.

The point we are making is that with just the simplest sleight of hand, change in estimate, or accounting gimmickry, a company's value can magically increase, often in a significant manner. In the previous scenarios, we have increased the cash flow multiple the company may receive on its annual cash flow from 7.6 to 17.5 to establish an estimated value (more than

EXHIBIT 15.2   DTC Business Unaudited Company Valuation Comparison

Unaudited - Prepared by Company Management

XYZ DtoC Example, Inc. Estimated Company Value - Comparison as of the Fiscal Year Ending 12/31/2020

Summary Income Statement - EBITDA	FYE	Scenario #1 Amount	Scenario #2 Amount	Scenario #3 Amount
Scenario A - Annual Earnings Growth Rate		8.00%	12.00%	16.00%
EBITDA, Actual FYE 12/31/20	12/31/2020	$1,500,000	$1,500,000	$1,800,000
Discount Rate Applied to Future Cash Flows		12.00%	9.00%	6.00%
Estimated or Implied Company Value		$11,400,000	$15,600,000	$26,300,000
Equivalent Cash Flow Multiple (based on base EBITDA)		7.60	10.40	17.53

Confidential - Property of XYZ DtoC Example, Inc.

	Counter	Amount	Amount	Amount
	1	$1,500,000	$1,500,000	$1,800,000
	2	$1,620,000	$1,680,000	$2,088,000
	3	$1,749,600	$1,881,600	$2,422,080
	4	$1,889,568	$2,107,392	$2,809,613
	5	$2,040,733	$2,360,279	$3,259,151
	6	$2,203,992	$2,643,513	$3,780,615
	7	$2,380,311	$2,960,734	$4,385,513
	8	$2,570,736	$3,316,022	$5,087,196
	9	$2,776,395	$3,713,945	$5,901,147
	10	$2,998,507	$4,159,618	$6,845,330
		$11,433,147	$15,597,192	$26,339,802

doubling the value). We would like to note that there is nothing inherently fraudulent or illegal with these valuation scenarios as, let us face it, an educated buyer and seller should execute an arm's-length transaction and agree on the fair market value of the business. But again, we refer to our statement that accounting is as much an art form as a science, which is often on full display when valuing a business. If the seller can convince (a term to be used carefully) the buyer that the adjusted EBITDA is in fact $1.8 million, the earnings growth rate will be north of 15%, and the risks associated with the business justify a lower discount rate, well then, more power to them and congratulations on driving such a high valuation.

At this point it should become obvious that to increase a business's value, two primary strategies are available. First is to increase or improve operating profits or cash flows through either (1) presenting forecasts that are, shall we say, very rosy and optimistic or (2) preparing proforma financial statements that display just how much historical EBITDA would be generated had unnecessary expenses been eliminated, economies of scales realized (through the combined businesses), and so on.

These adjustments are often referred to as *addbacks* and there are countless ways to document and support improvements in earnings and cash flows, some of which are legitimate and others of which are very much a reach, but the base logic remains the same; that is, to drive a higher value, selling businesses will make every effort to present the best possible operating results.

If the first strategy is to increase EBITDA (historical or future), then it makes sense that the second strategy would be to decrease the discount rate, which is nothing more than a reflection of perceived risk in a business.

That is, if an acquiring company sees higher levels of risk within the business, including such items as elevated competitive threats, slowing revenue growth rates, poor brand placement, lack of intellectual property protection, and a decaying management team (just to name a few), it will need an increased return on the acquisition investment, which translates into a higher discount rate (or lower valuation multiple). The higher perceived risk and threats to the business's economic model and ability to generate positive earnings will almost always result in lower multiples and reduced business value. For selling companies, the ability to proactively manage various operating risk factors and convince (for lack of a better term) the acquiring company that these risk factors are contained and/or insignificant and will not have a material impact on operating results moving forward represents a critical element of carefully planning for and structuring an acquisition.

CLOSING COMMENTS AND A CAUTIONARY WORD ABOUT THE FED!

Most people have heard the adage about real estate in that its value is determined based on three criteria – location, location, and location. The same logic can be held when buying and selling a business but, unlike location, the three criteria are timing, timing, and timing.

Obviously, there are many more factors that come into play when valuing and selling a business but when the stars align between the market conditions being ideal, the discount/interest rates being low, limited perceived economic risk, the financial performance of a company peaking (e.g., sales growth rates are still accelerating), and the proper packaging and presentation of the company to the market, the perceived value of a business can literally double or triple depending on nothing more than being in the right place at the right time. This applies to whether a company is looking to sell its business, raise capital, or undertake an IPO.

Closing out our discussion on how businesses are valued, we cannot resist the temptation to direct your attention to the Federal Reserve Bank and their current monetary policy. As previously noted, the Federal Reserve Bank has set short-term interest rates at just above zero, resulting in a current interest rate on the 10-year Treasury note of approximately 1.5%. If monetary policy is ever normalized and rates are increased to even the 3% to 4% range (which is still extremely low from a historical perspective), even a small change in a discount rate can have a huge impact on the value of a business. Not only is the Federal Reserve Bank encouraging companies to take out loans at extremely low interest rates (and thus helping companies reduce interest expense) but, in addition, they are artificially inflating company valuations via driving key interest rate benchmarks (the most important being the 10-year Treasury note rate) well below market or natural levels. If this ever reverses, you can begin to imagine the potential damage, as values for basically all long-term assets, including residential real estate, commercial real estate, stocks and bonds, commodities, and so on, will be negatively impacted. Suddenly, a loan-to-value ratio established for a commercial real estate property implodes, resulting in a covenant violation and the loan potentially being called. Can you say, *Ouch*, thank you very much? Our question to the Federal Reserve Bank is simple: How is the current monetary policy ever unwound without inflicting significant damage to the economy? Good luck with that.

Business Acquisitions – The Basics

TYPES OF BUSINESS ACQUISITIONS

Chapter 15 covered two primary subjects: *why* businesses are valued and the basics of *how* business valuations are determined. One of the key *whys* of a business valuation has to do with the owners of a company looking to realize a liquidity event. This represents a quite common event, as in today's high-intensity economy, more and more businesses are being formed, capitalized, built, and eventually positioned to be sold for a (hopefully) significant liquidity event, and in a relatively quick time period. For the purposes of this chapter, our discussion will be centered around more traditional business acquisitions from both the seller's and buyer's perspectives.

It is impossible to discuss all the attributes associated with a business acquisition, as documenting the legal issues alone would entail writing another book. So, to start this chapter, we focus on the two basic types of business acquisitions and offer some tax matters for consideration.

At a macro level, business acquisitions tend to come in one of two types:

1. *Asset deals* are generally structured around purchasing only the business assets of value (to the acquirer). In a number of cases, this may be all of the target company's assets and operations and in other cases, it may

be that the acquirer is simply interested in just a portion of the target company. Under an asset deal, specific assets of a business are acquired, with the remaining legal entity left intact to either wrap up its affairs or continue with other business operations. This process may include buying just the ongoing business operations (including inventory, property, plant, and equipment), as well as the intangible assets (customer lists, patents, trade names), and leaving the remaining assets, such as trade receivables, prepaid expenses, and cash, with the old legal entity. The acquiring company purchases the assets and then integrates them into their operation for the purpose of realizing economic gain. The selling company is left to finalize its business affairs by liquidating the remaining assets, paying off the creditors, and hopefully having a return available to the owners or shareholders. Asset deals tend to be associated with smaller, closely held, private companies.

In certain situations, the selling company may still have an ongoing operation intact as the sale may only involve one division or segment of the business. Hence, the selling business continues its operations as usual except for having one less division to worry about.

2. *Equity deals,* on the other hand, are generally based on purchasing the entire business entity (including buying all assets and assuming all liabilities). Under an equity deal, instead of purchasing specific assets of the selling company, the stock or equity of the selling company is purchased at fair market value, with all assets being acquired and all liabilities assumed. The acquired company usually survives as a legal entity and continues to operate as a subsidiary of the acquiring company or is in some capacity merged into a new entity formed for the specific purpose of acquiring the target company. Generally, the equity holders of the acquired company sell their holdings (stock, LLC membership interests, and so on) for cash, equity, or stock in the acquiring company, a note payable, or a combination of these items. Stock deals tend to be associated with larger, more complex, publicly traded companies (as well as the larger privately held businesses) that have ample liquid resources and freely traded stock to complete the transaction.

A quick point of emphasis on the income taxation front: Significant tax benefit and savings opportunities for both the buyer and the seller can be realized by structuring a business acquisition correctly. The most significant benefit (to the seller) is being able to realize a gain on the sale of a business using federally established long-term capital gains tax rates as opposed to short-term ordinary income tax rates or, better yet, structuring a transaction that allows the gain to be deferred from income taxes. Further, if the selling company has been legally structured as a Subchapter S corporation or LLC (which are tax pass-through entities), the gain on the sale of assets can be "passed through" to the owners of the entity and only taxed at the individual level, thus eliminating a common problem with asset sales in a C corporation (which can trigger a double taxation, once at the company level and once at the owner level).

 For the buyer, being able to properly allocate the purchase price of the acquisition to different assets that can be depreciated or amortized quicker may assist in reducing future income tax obligations, which ultimately lowers expenses and helps improve internal cash flows (but this may come at a cost to the seller). There is no way we can possibly cover all the potential tax savings and planning opportunities so rather we will leave you with this bit of advice: ***Obtaining proper professional accounting, legal, and taxation advice during the acquisition process represents an essential element of any business acquisition or sale and should be included in the planning process from the very beginning.***

Although several advantages and disadvantages are present with each acquisition type, the same premise usually holds under either transaction in that the general business interests of the acquired company are maintained on an ongoing basis because the acquisition was based on the premise that an economically viable operation is present.

BUSINESS VALUATION ADJUSTMENTS

Chapter 15 provided an overview on how businesses are valued to calculate a gross enterprise value. The gross enterprise value does not take into consideration how a company has been financed (with debt or equity), nor does it account for any other valuation adjustments that an acquiring company may want to capture (because of perceived risks, uncertainties, or opportunities). In this section, a brief summary of common business valuations adjustments is provided to help the reader understand the difference between the total or gross enterprise value and the actual net consideration paid when a business is acquired.

For this discussion, we assume that a business valuation has been completed for an exit/liquidity event or to raise capital. Referring to Exhibit 15.2, you can see that the total or gross business enterprise value was estimated to be $26.3 million using scenario 3. This value includes all tangible, intangible, and other assets that are necessary to generate the agreed-upon EBITDA. While the gross enterprise value has been set at $26.3 million, the net value paid at closing will be adjusted for the following items (which are common adjustments in a business acquisition).

> *Net working capital (NWC):* The selling company guarantees that a minimum NWC level will be present at the date of closing. In most cases, the NWC is calculated by taking total trade receivables, inventory, and other current assets, less trade payables, accrued liabilities, and other normal and recurring current liabilities. For example, if the selling company is guaranteeing that $3.5 million of NWC will be present but only delivers $3.0 million, then at the closing date, a deduction in the proceeds of $500,000 will be realized.

> *Cash-free/debt-free:* Acquisitions often include a concept referred to as cash-free/debt-free. That is, if a company has excess cash available at the date of closing, it can elect to distribute it to the owners prior to closing. Also, when the term *debt-free* is used, it means the acquisition is being completed with no loans or notes payable included (which are the responsibility of the selling company to pay in full, usually upon closing the transaction).

> *Loans and notes payable:* Acquiring companies may or may not assume outstanding loans or notes payable as part of the transaction. The decision to assume debt is dependent on the unique elements of each transaction but for smaller transactions, generally debt is not assumed (by the acquiring company); rather, enough funds from the acquisition price are earmarked or set aside to ensure that the debt is paid in full. The reason for this is based in the fact that most loans or notes payable have a priority or secured position against the assets of the selling company so for the acquiring company to get free and clear ownership of all assets, the existing loans must be paid in full. In the case of the acquiring company assuming any outstanding loans or notes payable, the value of this debt is almost always deducted from the gross enterprise value to calculate the net value and consideration to be paid.

> *Other holdbacks:* Finally, a wide range of other adjustments or holdbacks may be built into an acquisition that impact the net consideration

received (by the seller). These holdbacks are dependent on perceived risks that may involve unsettled litigation, a dispute over intellectual property ownership, potential long-term commitments and contingencies that will need to be satisfied, and so on.

The point being made is that when you hear or read about a business being valued for X millions of dollars, the actual net value received by the selling company (from the acquisition) could be far less as a result of the above-mentioned adjustments (or others). Therefore, it is not uncommon to hear about large acquisitions or mergers that value a company at multibillions of dollars but also then disclose how much debt was assumed, resulting in a net acquisition price being less.

TYPES OF CONSIDERATION RECEIVED

As we continue to move through our discussion, starting with why a business was valued, how it was valued, what type of acquisition was utilized, and the adjustments made to the gross enterprise value, we now reach the all-important point of realizing what consideration will be received. It may come as a surprise that for most business acquisitions, a combination of cash, equity, and other forms of consideration is received, as 100% cash deals are generally the exception and not the norm.

> ➤ *Cash:* Most business acquisitions incorporate a significant percentage of the net purchase price in the form of cash for various reasons. By offering cash, the seller generally becomes more motivated to complete the transaction as the thought of receiving equity, earnouts, and so on and not having any liquidity at the close of the transaction is not appealing. Most sophisticated buyers know they need to offer cash to help entice the seller and in addition, may not want to offer 100% of the acquisition in the form of stock from their company (as it could dilute existing ownership). There are no set rules as to the amount of cash consideration at closing but ranges of 50% to 80% of the net purchase price are common.

> ➤ *Equity:* Equity in the acquiring company is often used as part of the consideration in a business acquisition (e.g., the seller will receive 20% of the purchase price in the buyer's stock, which represents X

shares based on the value at the closing date). The buyer may utilize an equity element to help conserve their cash, make sure the seller has continued "skin in the game" (to keep them motivated to ensure that the acquisition proceeds smoothly), or might want to use their stock if its value is at a high level (as they can issue fewer shares that are more valuable). For the seller, receiving equity might be appealing in relation to deferring taxable gains (if the transaction qualifies for a like-kind exchange as defined by the IRS) and being able to participate in a second bite of the apple, assuming the equity received increases in value over the coming years. However, receiving equity also comes with risks, including not being able to sell the stock if needed (because of the acquiring company being private or requiring restrictive lock-up periods on how soon stock can be sold after the acquisition) or bearing a risk of loss if the acquiring company's value drops. Like cash, there are no set rules on how much equity might be offered as part of an acquisition and is dependent on the appetite and desires of both the buyer and seller.

➤ *Notes payable:* In certain cases, a buyer may request that the seller take a note payable as part of the consideration (this is often referred to as carrying back a note). For example, a company may be acquired for $20 million and the buyer wants to pay $15 million at closing and thus requests the seller to carry back a note payable for $5 million (to be paid out over three years). For the buyer, having the seller help finance the acquisition may be appealing, as it helps conserve cash and keeps the seller actively involved in the business. The downside, of course, is that the buyer is issuing debt and must pay interest on the note. For the seller, it might be appealing to receive a portion of the consideration over a period (to ensure a consistent income stream) as well as possibly being able to defer a portion of the taxable gain over a period of time (maybe in a lower future income tax year). But with the pros come the cons as for the seller, risks abound in relation to now having to rely on the buyer to service the debt (and remit periodic principal and interest payments), not to mention the fact that the note carried back by the seller will most likely be structured in a junior or subordinated position (lower in payment priority to senior debt, thus basically being the lowest on the totem pole).

➤ *The earnout:* A variation of carrying back a note payable on the transaction is the dreaded *earnout*. We use the term *dreaded* because earnouts can really get messy for both the buyer and the seller. Basically, what an earnout represents is the lowest form and structure of a note payable supporting the acquisition but one that is not guaranteed. With a note payable, the terms are generally set (i.e., you will receive X dollars every month for Y years). With an earnout, the payments to the seller are only made if certain pre-agreed-upon milestones are met after the acquisition is completed (e.g., if the company generates Y sales for the next two years, you will get Z additional dollars). Earnouts can be based on a variety of milestones that are generally centered on financial milestones such as sales revenue, gross profits, or operating profits. This of course is where it can get messy, as the definitions, interpretations, and calculations of the earnout milestones can become problematic (as business conditions may change after the acquisition). You can probably see why a buyer would want to utilize an earnout as it helps reduce risks and keeps the seller highly motivated to stay engaged (and earn their remaining consideration). For a seller, you can see why this is not appealing, as any number of things may go wrong, jeopardizing the future earnout payment; but in some cases, when uncertainties are present, incorporating an earnout into the acquisition may represent the only viable solution to complete the deal.

➢ *Assumed debt (limited but a real form of consideration):* Using the previous example, if a company's gross enterprise value is set at $26.3 million but the company has outstanding loans totaling $8.3 million, the acquiring company could assume the $8.3 million of loans and then at closing, $18 million of other consideration (e.g., cash, acquiring company equity, etc.) would be transferred to the sellers. There are several factors that go into determining whether a company would or can assume outstanding debt (of the seller) or simply make sure the debt is paid. As a rule of thumb, the larger and more complex transactions, which are usually structured as an equity deal, tend to include debt assumption structures, whereas smaller and simpler transactions usually look to make sure the debt is paid at closing.

Quite often, it is easier for the seller and the buyer to agree on the value of a company than on the final structure of the transaction, including what forms of consideration will be received. It is one thing to determine that a company is worth $XXX, but it is something entirely different to actually receive $XXX.

Strategically, it is worth noting the following from both the seller's and the buyer's perspectives to help manage risks associated with a transaction.

> ➤ **Seller:** The agreed-upon value is important, but making sure you are comfortable with the cash consideration received is critical. In a sense, you almost must have a mindset that if the deal blows up after the closing and you do not receive any additional consideration, the cash component was enough to cover a good (but not great) value for the business and provide a proper return (in relation to the risks taken to build the business). When additional forms of consideration are present, including receiving equity in the acquiring entity or accepting an earnout, the seller may want to view these as icing on the cake (for lack of a better term), as what the seller is basically doing is betting on the ongoing business and management team to deliver an additional return. The importance of completing reverse due diligence (i.e., when the seller evaluates the merits and qualifications of the buying entity) cannot be emphasized enough.

> ➤ **Buyer:** The buyer, like the seller, must be comfortable with the valuation, even if it is on the high side, as hedges are available to help manage perceived risks. To start, the buyer could utilize an earnout component, an equity stake in the acquiring entity (with restrictions), or include notes payable to help finance the transaction. By using these acquisition structuring strategies, the buyer can achieve two goals. First, the buyer can conserve cash and (hopefully) manage the cash generated from the acquisition against future payments (on notes or earnouts). This allows the buyer to match long-term cash inflows against future long-term cash outflows. Second, by utilizing equity stakes or earnouts, the sellers should be more motivated to remain involved with the ongoing business to ensure its success (and to reap additional consideration or, as they like to say when issuing equity, getting a chance to take a second bite of the apple when an additional liquidity event occurs).

ADDITIONAL BUSINESS ACQUISITION TIPS AND TIDBITS

There is simply no way to cover all the terms, strategies, complexities, and nuances associated with buying and selling a business in one book, let alone one chapter. The goal with presenting this material was to provide a macro-level overview on business acquisitions, especially given just how important buying and selling businesses (or portions of businesses) have become in today's global market. As we close our discussion on business acquisitions, we offer these additional thoughts on the intangible component of the business acquisition process:

> ➤ ***Prepare the product:*** Your company should be very well prepared, packaged, and presented to the market (this starts well before the final deal closing). The company's story, quality of financial and operational information, presentation deck, and internal team committed to the process need to be exceptional. Further, sellers need to make sure that it is the right time to exit and that everyone (i.e., owners, management, founders, etc.) is ready to sell.

> ➤ ***Qualify the parties and market:*** Be it a buyer looking at acquiring a company or a seller looking to exit, everyone needs to qualify the opposite party in terms of their real capabilities to close a transaction efficiently and effectively. There is no need to waste anyone's time engaging with unqualified parties. Also, we would like to emphasize the importance of market timing, as if the economic tides turn, there is no point in pitching an opportunity when nobody's listening.

> ➤ ***Assemble your team:*** Buyers or sellers, make sure you have the right professional resources, including legal, taxation, financial, accounting, technology, operational, marketing, and so forth to support the process. Investment bankers are often extremely valuable in the process to ensure that the right parties are brought together.

> ➤ ***Market the product:*** If you don't make calls, you don't make sales, but, in this case, make sure the right calls are made to the right parties in a smart, efficient, and protected manner. By protected, we mean that any information sharing between different parties is done at the right time, in the proper format, and protected by NDAs (nondisclosure agreements) or CAs (confidentiality agreements). To be honest, most companies selling their businesses already know who the potential buyers will be given their business and industry knowledge.

> ➤ ***Diligence and negotiations:*** This portion of the acquisition process (assuming you make it this far) is generally incredibly detailed, lengthy, time-consuming (requiring management's attention), and can be frustrating if you are not prepared. This goes for both parties but especially the selling entity as diligence can be thought of as being the equivalent of receiving a colonoscopy.

➢ **Reps and warranties (R&Ws):** Finally, it is imperative that both the buyer and the seller understand the importance, risks, and value associated with reps and warranties. R&Ws are statements that the buyer or seller will make in the final closing documents that confirm an understanding of the parties. For example, a buyer will ask a seller to make an R&W that they are not aware of any pending litigation that may negatively impact the business. The list of R&Ws that can be included in an agreement is extensive and can easily exceed 50 or more (in a medium-sized transaction), but the idea is to ensure that both parties are being as truthful, honest, and transparent as possible. We should also add that R&Ws can be used as a negotiating tool that in some capacity can be structured to exchange value for loosening a specific R&W that has a higher perceived risk. But be careful, as this can be a tightrope to walk because if a buyer sees the seller balking at too many R&Ws, they may get spooked.

CHAPTER 17

Deciphering the Cap Table

CRITICAL KNOWLEDGE TO HELP MAINTAIN CONTROL OF YOUR BUSINESS

Here we are, at the end of the book. Fittingly, we have elected to hold our final discussion to the last section of the balance sheet – owner's or stockholders' equity. This is the section of the balance sheet that appears on the bottom of the right-hand side of the balance sheet (from a horizontal perspective) or at the bottom of the second page (from a vertical perspective). It is no coincidence that we have saved this topic for the end of the book as, after all is said and done with learning the *whats*, *whens*, *wheres*, and *hows* of financial information, we turn our attention to *who* owns and controls a business (and why this is so critical, beyond the obvious reasons).

Before we dive into explaining owners' equity in more depth, we would like to preface our discussion by highlighting two points:

1. For those readers who are operating a business unit or division of an existing business, our discussion on owners' equity and business capitalization may not appear to be all that relevant (why bother? The corporate mother ship deals with the function of raising capital and

managing the owners and creditors). Simple enough, but we should note that the topics covered in this chapter could be useful for you to understand beyond just how your organization is capitalized. It is important to clearly understand that whether it be working with customers, suppliers, strategic partners, or the like, the ownership of any third party can have a huge influence on future decision-making (and your relationship with these parties).

2. Most small businesses tend to be closely held and formed as either partnerships, Subchapter S corporations, or simple single-owner limited liability companies (LLCs). For these entities, owners' equity is often an afterthought, as the net equity of these types of businesses is usually just comprised of two components, retained earnings and common equity. For these types of companies, retained earnings are nothing more than a business's cumulative net profits and losses, less any distributions of earnings paid (made over the year). Common equity captures the amount of capital contributed by the owners of the company who generally (and legally) should have the same rights to profits, distributions, voting, and so forth on a prorated basis to their actual ownership. That is, if one owner invested $20,000 in exchange for 2,000 common stock shares and another owner invested $10,000 in exchange for 1,000 common stock shares, the first owner should maintain rights to distributions of earnings, profits, and voting of 66.67% (2,000 shares owned out of 3,000 shares issued in total). Again, and by reading on, you as a small business owner will gain additional knowledge that may be useful when dealing with third parties or, better yet, if considering raising more complex forms of capital (and their pros and cons).

Our discussion on owners' equity is going to move well beyond smaller businesses and be directed toward more complex business capital structures that involve multiple types of equity and even quasi forms of equity disguised as debt. While all businesses will have retained earnings (as previously discussed) or, in the case of multiple years of losses, accumulated deficits (where cumulative losses are greater than cumulative profits), when companies utilize more complex legal entities such as C corporations or multi-owner LLCs they also tend to use a wider range of different types of equity to capitalize their business. In a nutshell, this is what is commonly referred to as the capitalization table or (*cap table*).

The cap table is really nothing more than a table or spreadsheet that spells out exactly who owns what in terms of the equity issued by a company as presented or listed by what type of equity has been issued. On the surface, reading a cap table should be relatively straightforward, as it should list various parties and their respective ownership percentage in the company's owner equity. However, as previously discussed, the devil is absolutely in the details when understanding cap tables and the potential impact as to what owners truly control the company and have the most advantageous ownership stakes.

We have laid out the topics covered in this chapter from the perspective of the equity owner's rights to claims against the company as opposed to the total amount of equity owned in the company. This may seem somewhat convoluted, but as you read through the material you will quickly gain an understanding of why it is important to understate rights and preferences in lockstep with total ownership interest. For simplicity, our discussion focuses on three main components of a typical cap table:

1. Risk-based debt (e.g., convertible notes)
2. Preferred equity
3. Common equity, options, and warrants

Before we dive into these topics in more depth, a quick word is warranted on the primary available sources of equity capital (from the market). Raising equity can be achieved by pursuing different sources of capital ranging from tapping what we like to refer to as FF&CBAs (family, friends, and close business associates), who are often unsophisticated when making investment decisions, all the way to taking a company public through an IPO (a complex process targeting sophisticated investors).

In between these two extremes is equity capital, which is usually raised from groups that have a keen expertise in providing the right financial capital at the right time and include VCs (venture capitalists), PEs or PEGs (private equity or private equity groups), HNWIs (high-net-worth individuals, sometimes referred to as angel investors), HFs (hedge funds), and other similar types of capital sources. These groups tend to specialize by industry or company stage, usually have significant amounts of capital to deploy, and employ highly qualified management teams to assess the investment opportunities.

EQUITY DISGUISED AS DEBT

Companies that cannot raise capital from traditional debt sources, such as banks or alternative-based lenders, and which do not want to raise equity capital (over fears of diluting the ownership and control of the company) will often use what is commonly referred to as convertible debt (a hybrid form of debt and equity that has characteristics of both).

Convertible debt is a form of actual debt (i.e., a loan to the company) that is reported on a company's balance sheet as a liability, similar to a note or loan payable. Most convertible debt is structured to be long term, with common repayment terms of two to five years. The reason for the name is that convertible debt, either at the option of the party providing the loan or if a specific event occurs, can be converted into either common or preferred equity of the company. The conversion of the debt may occur for any number of reasons, including the company achieving a milestone such as a predetermined sales revenue level being met or, if the company raises a large amount of equity (the triggering event), the company is sold, or if the due date of the convertible debt is reached and the debt cannot be repaid.

Two logical questions at this point are, why would a company want to raise money using convertible debt, and, conversely, why would an external party want to invest in convertible debt? We answer both questions as follows:

1. ***Issuing convertible debt to raise capital:*** Raising capital through issuing convertible debt is often used by companies that need to bridge the business (by providing a capital infusion) to get from point D to point F to help substantiate a higher valuation. If a company is worth $X at point D but can see it being worth three times more at point F (based on achieving key milestones), the company will be able to raise equity capital at a much higher valuation and reduce the risk of ownership dilution. Further, when a company does not qualify for traditional bank or alternative-based loans, it can tap a more junior or subordinated type of debt by raising capital through convertible debt (and if structured correctly by the company, it can avoid providing an actual secured interest in company assets).

    Convertible debt, just like traditional bank loans, will be required to pay interest and have set repayment terms the company must abide by but, generally speaking, the repayment terms are structured very favorably for the company. That is, a below-market interest rate is provided, which is accrued monthly and not paid until the due date of the convertible debt. Further, it is not uncommon for convertible debt to not require periodic payments but come 100% due at the end of the term. Under this structure, the company has the maximum flexibility to use the capital raised for the longest period of time (as the debt interest and principal will not be due until the very end).

2. ***Investing in convertible debt to provide capital:*** So why would a convertible debt investment be of interest to third parties? Here is your answer: First up, debt has a higher seniority or claim against company assets than equity. Although convertible debt is often structured in a junior position to bank or alternative lender loans (i.e., these lenders have a higher claim to company assets in case of a company liquidation or bankruptcy, so they get paid first, assuming cash is available), they sit higher in the "cap stack" as it relates to distributing company assets in the event of an unfortunate or depressed company sale. Second, the convertible debt investors can earn a set return on their investments from the interest rate established (such as 6% per annum), even though this may not be paid until the due date.

Third, and maybe most importantly, the convertible debt investors have additional return upside via being able to convert into the company's equity down the road. It is quite common for convertible debt to include a feature that allows the investors to convert into the company's equity at a discount to a future capital raise. For example, the convertible debt investors may be provided a 20% discount against the price of company's equity value established in a large subsequent equity capital raise. If the company raised a large amount of capital at $20 per share, the convertible debt investors would be allowed to convert the debt principal and any accrued interest at $16 per share (thus realizing an additional 20% return on their invested capital).

Similar to convertible debt, a company may raise capital through issuing a junior tranche of debt that has set repayment terms and interest rates established. But unlike convertible debt, warrants to purchase equity in the company may be attached instead of allowing the debt to convert. For example, if our sample company needed to sweeten the deal to entice the third-party lender to provide the loan of $8 million, it could offer the lender a warrant to purchase 50,000 common shares at $1 per share at the lender's choice. Similar to the 20% discount provided to the investors in the convertible debt, the common stock warrant provides for an "equity kicker" to enhance the overall investment return well above the stated interest rate.

The nuances, details, and specifics surrounding convertible or junior debt are extensive and complex and well beyond the scope of this book. Our goal with overviewing this form of capital was not to make you an expert on this specific subject but rather to socialize the concept of debt/equity hybrid forms of capital and why they are attractive to both the company raising capital and the investors providing capital. In effect, these forms of capital represent a middle-of-the-road strategy to help balance the use of debt and equity in one type of financial capital. As with all forms of financial capital, there are pros and cons associated with each form, so the trick is knowing when to use each form and, in all cases, making sure you have proper professional counsel to navigate the capital-raising process.

PREFERRED EQUITY AND THE REAL CONTROL

We are now going to move further down the cap table and explore the wonderful world of preferred equity. Before we do this, let us look at where we stand in the investor priority list to make sure we understand the basic order of potential claims that creditors, investors, and owners would have against the company (in the event of a company liquidation, dissolution, or bankruptcy), which we touched on in the previous section when referring to the "cap stack." Exhibit 17.1 provides a simple summary of the cap stack for our sample company.

EXHIBIT 17.1   Unaudited Estimated Cap Stack

Unaudited - Prepared by Company Management

QW Example Tech., Inc.
Estimated Cap Stack
For the Fiscal Year Ending
12/31/2020

Summary of Liabilities & Equity	Priority Status	Amount	Notes/Comments
Payroll, Taxes, & Burden Payable	High	$451,000	Employee obligations are generally at the top of the list.
Income Taxes Payable	High	$523,000	Governments make sure they get their money.
Loans & Notes Payable, Secured	High	$8,000,000	Senior debt/secured against company assets.
Trade Payables & Accrued Liabilities	High/ Med.	$2,394,000	Depending on terms with vendors, could be high or medium.

Deferred Revenue & Other Current Lia.	Medium	$4,593,750	Customer advance payments and deposits not secured.
Other Long-Term Debt	Medium	$625,000	Other contingent debt, limited rights to assets.
Subtotal Liabilities		$16,586,750	
Preferred Stock	Med/Low	$8,000,000	Higher preference than common but lower than debt.
Common Stock	Low	$10,000,000	Basically last in priority with rights to company assets.
Common Stock Options & Warrants	Bottom	$0	Value dependent on successful company only.
Subtotal Shareholders' Equity		$18,000,000	
Total Liabilities & Equity		$34,586,750	

Confidential - Property of QW Example Tech., Inc.

Later in this chapter, we present our sample company's cap table in Exhibit 17.2, which emphasizes equity ownership (i.e., who owns what). The cap stack presented in Exhibit 17.1 emphasizes the pecking order of creditors', investors', and owners' claims against company assets and provides some comments and thoughts on who would get what in the liquidating event. It should be obvious that the cap stack can be a very sobering analysis for equity investors as, in this case, if the company had to liquidate and received $25 million for all its assets because of a forced liquidation proceeding, it would have enough to cover the total liabilities with just enough left over to repay the preferred stock owners (leaving nothing for the common stock owners).

The reason we presented the cap stack is to highlight the priority status of the preferred stock owners of being below debt but above common stock owners. This is the first and most critical concept to understand about preferred equity or stock: It almost always has a *preference* to common equity or stock when it comes to not just rights to dividends or earnings (before the common equity) but more importantly, claims against company assets. In our sample company, we previously disclosed that the preferred equity has the right to receive an 8% annual dividend before any company earnings are returned to common stock owners. The preferred equity investors also negotiated terms in this capital offering that include a 1.5x preference upon a liquidating event. What this means is that after all debt is satisfied, the preferred equity investors receive 150% of their capital investment (in this case $12 million) along with any earned but unpaid preferred stock dividends before the common stock owners receive anything (which is also referred to having a *first out* exit provision as their money is first out of the deal). And just to sweeten the deal further, the preferred equity investors included a provision that allows them to convert their preferred stock to common stock upon a qualified event (e.g., a company sale that achieves a specific exit value or a successful IPO).

The second critical concept to understand about preferred equity is that usually the investors demand a certain amount of management control, either directly or indirectly, with the company's affairs. For large, preferred capital raises, it is quite common for investors to demand a seat (or possibly two) on the board of directors. For a company that has five board members prior to the preferred capital raise, the terms of the raise may require that the board of directors increase to seven, of which two will be appointed by the preferred equity investors. There are clear reasons preferred equity investors demand board participation, including the ability for them to monitor their investment more closely, as well as to provide valuable executive management insight they may bring to the table. The point is that board of director participation represents direct strategic management involvement in the company.

Indirectly, the preferred investors can (and usually do) include several negative control provisions that help protect their investment. Examples of negative control provisions include requiring 100% board approval to raise capital through another equity offering (so that better terms cannot be offered to the next investors at the expense of the current preferred investors), limitations on how much and what type of loans or notes payable can be secured (without their approval), and 100% board authorization and approval in the event the company sells the majority of its business interests. Our examples could go on and on but by now you should get the picture loud and clear. When capital is raised in the form of preferred equity, the structure of these deals tends to strongly favor the preferred equity investors by providing significant financial preferences (to enhance their return) and management involvement (to protect and control their investments).

There is so much information and knowledge surrounding the subject of preferred equity that an entire book could be written on the terms, conditions, provisions, pros, cons, dos, don'ts, and I-should-have-known-betters. In closing, we would like to leave you with this perspective on preferred equity investments, specifically, how the financial community can put a spin on a company and inflate its value.

The financial community (especially VCs and PEGs) often make references to *unicorns*, which are nothing more than start-up or young companies that have achieved an extremely lofty valuation (usually $1 billion or more). The high valuation is derived from the fact that if a $100 million investment is made in a company that values the entire company at $1 billion, then the party(ies) making the investment own 10% of the company. Okay, simple enough, as somebody invested $100 million for a 10% stake in the company (so its value must be $1 billion).

What they do not tell you is that the $100 million investment was made in preferred equity that includes the protections discussed in this chapter. Hence, if the company is successful and sells for $2 billion, the preferred investors can convert their preferred shares into common shares, still owning 10% of the company, and sell out for $200 million. Not bad for the investment, as this is the story everyone wants to hear and achieve. But in the event the company struggles and is ultimately sold off the scrap heap for $250 million (still a tidy sum), the preferred investors do not get 10% or $25 million but rather are protected with a 1x preference and will get their $100 million back.

Remember this, as when you hear about unicorn valuations, this is the value the investors *hope* the company will be worth down the road (not necessarily what it is worth now) and, if it is not, well, they can cover their downside by investing in preferred equity with favorable terms. In other words, this is just more financial lingo and terminology to familiarize yourself with to make sure you understand the never-ending flow of bullshit oozing from the financial community.

COMMON EQUITY, OPTIONS, AND WARRANTS

Finally, we reach the end of the cap table and conclude our discussion by briefly discussing common stock ownership and common stock options or warrants. There is really not a lot to discuss, as the reference to "common" says it all. That is, with common stock, everyone is basically in the same bucket with rights to earnings, voting on company matters, claims against company assets, and similar matters. Larger companies may issue multiple types of common stock with a common feature being that the class A common stock has voting rights and the class B common stock has no voting rights, but this type of equity complexity is generally only found in the largest and most powerful companies (e.g., Alphabet, aka Google, Class A and C common stock).

Exhibit 17.2 presents our sample company's cap table, which now reflects ownership by what type of equity owns what percentage of the company.

EXHIBIT 17.2 Unaudited Cap Table

Unaudited - Prepared by Company Management

QW Example Tech., Inc.
Unaudited Cap Table
For the Fiscal Year Ending
12/31/2020

Description	Number of Shares	Invested Amount	Voting Issued & O/S % Owned	Fully Diluted % Owned
Preferred Equity:				
H&H Test VC Firm, Fund V	500,000	$8,000,000	33.33%	30.77%
Subtotal – Preferred Equity	500,000	$8,000,000	33.33%	30.77%
Common Equity:				
Founders, Original	800,000	$4,000,000	53.33%	49.23%
Investors, Various Parties	200,000	$6,000,000	13.33%	12.31%
Subtotal – Common Equity	1,000,000	$10,000,000	66.67%	61.54%
Common Equity Options & Warrants:				
Stock options issued & outstanding	75,000	$0	0.00%	4.62%
Warrants issued for common stock purchases	50,000	$0	0.00%	3.08%
Subtotal – Common Equity Options & Warrants	125,000	$0	0.00%	7.69%
Total, all forms of equity	1,625,000	$18,000,000	100.00%	100.00%

Confidential - Property of QW Example Tech., Inc.

The items of importance in the cap table are as follows:

➤ Two columns of ownership percentages have been provided, voting and fully diluted. Voting captures only the equity that is issued and outstanding that has voting rights. Since common stock options and warrants are nothing more than having rights to purchase common stock at a later date, they do not have voting rights (thus the reference to 0% ownership in this column). The fully diluted column calculates the ownership percentages of the company if all forms of equity were issued and outstanding and held equal rights.

➤ The cap table reconciles to the statement of change in stockholders' equity presented in Exhibit 9.1 but now presents the information in a different format (to help the investors understand where they rank in the cap table and the ownership percentages in the company).

➤ An item of significant importance is the voting ownership percentage of 53.33% controlled by the common equity group referenced as "founders." This indicates that the founders of the company still control a majority of the voting shares (just over 50%) and, at least through the most recent preferred capital raise, still retain management control of the company (which is especially important for obvious reasons).

➤ Completing a little bit of math, you can calculate that the new preferred equity investors purchased their shares at $16 each compared to the original founders investing at $5 per common share and the other common stock owners at $30 per share. In other words, the preferred equity investors are breaking even, the original founders' shares have increased in value, while the other common equities investors are currently holding the bag (with implied losses). Oh, well, not every investment turns out to be a winner (at least based on the current valuation), but the other common equity investors are hopeful that management, by implementing its new business plan, can increase the value of the company so that all investors achieve a positive return on their investments.

➤ The final item in the cap table captures the issuance of equity incentive grants in the form of common stock options or warrants. Common stock options and warrants are often issued (with the right to exercise at a set price based on a future event) to key employees, board members, strategic third parties, and others to provide an extra monetary incentive to allow these parties to participate in the increase in a company's value (if all goes well). Almost all large companies utilize these types of incentives to attract top employee talent and keep parties engaged with the business to help build value and achieve a successful exit. If all goes well, everyone makes out and if it does not, let us just say that more than a few common stock options have turned out to be worthless. Options and warrants may have value to the recipient (eventually), but they only provide an option to purchase so unless the option is exercised, these types of equity have no rights to earnings and cannot vote. Thus, we place them at the very bottom of the cap table, as this group of (potential) equity owners are truly last in line.

 We have reached the bottom of the food chain as it relates to rights to both earnings and claims against assets. It may seem counterintuitive that the founders and the early other common equity investors along with key insiders (in control of common stock options and warrants), the ones that have poured their blood, sweat, and tears into building the business, stand last in line, but this is the reality of operating a business and building it into something of real value. When you raise capital and ask other parties to believe in your business, you must remember the golden rule: Whoever has the gold makes the rules!

OUR FINAL RAISING CAPITAL TIPS, TIDBITS, AND TRAPS

Closing our discussion on raising capital as well as the entire book, we would like to leave you with these words of wisdom.

- ➤ *First, cash is king.* Businesses must proactively, appropriately, and prudently manage cash resources or, to paraphrase the words of Warden Norton from the movie *Shawshank Redemption* (referring to the escape of Andy Dufresne), "Lord, it's a miracle, he just vanished like a fart in the wind." If not responsibly managed and protected, your cash will vanish like a fart in the wind!
- ➤ *Second, never run out of cash.* It is somewhat easy to discuss a miss or negative variance in the income statement, especially if you have best-in-class information (to explain the miss). But if you run out of cash and must explain this to an investor/lender, get ready to have a rather unpleasant discussion with your capital sources as it is going to be painful and most likely involve some very restrictive and unfavorable terms (if they even consider providing more capital).
- ➤ *Third, when capital sources offer extra cash, take it!* Yes, this may translate into more ownership dilution and/or added interest expense, but the ability to build a liquidity cushion for when a business hits the

eventual speed bump (which you will), is invaluable. There is nothing worse than having to raise cash when times are tough.

➤ *Fourth, timing can be everything.* Companies will look to offer equity when the price is high (to limit ownership dilution). This is a quite common tactic with large, hot companies looking to raise extra cash for use down the road as evidenced by Tesla in 2020 (raising extra capital). You will need to pay close attention to economic and market cycles, which can change quickly.

➤ *Fifth, when cash is tight, know your balance sheet and how to squeeze it.* You could incentivize customers to pay early or make deposits (e.g., a strategy used by Tesla) or push your vendors a bit (but not too much). You might also be able to work with key lenders or investors to have a bit of a slush fund to tap when needed. The key is to plan proactively, understand your cash flow statement, and communicate effectively.

- Sixth, and most importantly, understand that who you take capital from is often more important than the amount, type, and structure of that capital. Having the right financial partners that understand your business and timelines and have vast experience and resources can be invaluable. Securing capital from the right source can really help turn a highly stressful process into a wonderful experience. Secure capital from the wrong source and get ready for hell.

In summary – and yes, for the last time – we emphasize the importance of understanding and relying on the statement of cash flows and retaining proper levels of liquidity to operate your business in good times or bad. There is nothing worse than having to tap capital markets in a hostile environment as the terms will most likely be ugly (if you get them at all). Also remember the adage about banks: They will lend when you do not need it and when you do, they are nowhere to be found.

Index